CHRISTS VOICE TO LONDON.

AND
the Great Day of Gods Wrath.

Being the Substance of

II. Sermons

Preached (in the CITY) in the time of the sad VISITATION.

Together with the Necessity of Watching and Praying.

With a small Treatise of DEATH.

By WILLIAM DYER, a Servant of JESUS CHRIST.

The Lords voice cryeth to the City, Mich. 6. 9.

LONDON, Printed for E. Calvert, and are to be sold at the Black-spread Eagle near the West end of Pauls, 1666.

[To] the Inhabitants of the Parish of St. *Ann Aldersgate* in the City of LONDON,

Greeting:

[...] and Peace be multiplied unto you, [thro]ugh the knowledge of God, and of [Je]sus our Lord.

[Be]loved,

THE ever blessed God in the creating of Man, had a twofold End;
[A] Gracious End,
[A]nd a Glorious End.
[He] ought Ministers to have a [two]fold End;
[The] Glory of God,
[A]nd, the Good of Souls.

A 3   These

The Epistle

These Ends had I in the p[rea]-
ching of these Sermons to y[ou,]
and now also in the Printin[g of]
them for you.

Forasmuch as I was desire[d by]
some of you, to come & pr[each]
publickly amongst you, w[ith-]
out any opposition or im[posi-]
tion; to which I condescen[ded,]
hoping thereby to bring g[lory]
to God, and good to your [souls,]
without having the least tho[ught]
of publishing to the W[orld]
what I then preached to y[ou.]

But having since been ear[nest-]
ly importuned, and much [desi-]
red by several Friends, to [print]
them for publick Benefit, I [have]
accordingly answered the[ir de-]
sires.

And because these tw[o]

Dedicatory.

...ons were preached publikely
...mongst you, I thought it my
...ty also to dedicate them unto
...u, that what your ears let
...p in the hearing of them,
...ur eyes may regain by the
...ding of them.

Dear Friends, I hope these
...mons will not be the less ac-
...pted by you, because they
...me in a plain dress: I confess
...ere is more of heart in them,
...an Art: I hope the less man
...peareth in them, the more
...od will appear by them; who
...any times maketh use of
...ak Means, to effect great
...ds; *For out of the mouth of*
...bes and Sucklings, hast thou or-
...ned strength, Psal. 8. 2. And for
...s our dear Lord thanks his
                    Father,

A 4

The Epistle

Father, in *Matt.* 11. 25. I th[ank]
thee, O Father, Lord of H[eaven]
and Earth, because thou ha[st hid]
these things from the wise and [pru]
dent, and hast revealed them [unto]
Babes. Ver. 26. Even so Father,
so it seemed good in thy sight. So [else]
where it is said, To you it is gi[ven]
to know the Mysteries of the K[ing]
dom of Heaven; but unto them [it is]
not given.

    Friends, I may say to you, [as]
the blessed Apostle Paul said [to]
the Corinthians, My speech, and [my]
preaching, was not with enti[cing]
words of mans wisdom, but in [de]
monstration of the Spirit and of [pow]
er, that your Faith might not [stand]
in the wisdom of men, but in [the]
power of God; 1 Cor. 2. 4, 5. [And]
none that heard me (or sh[all]

Dedicatory.

...me) will think I spake too ...ch, or too home. O my ...ends! can a man speak too ...ch for God and his glory? ...n a man speak too much a-...inst sin and wickedness? Or, ...n a man speak too much for ...e eternal good of souls, which ...e more worth than a world? ...r what will it profit a man ...o gain the whole world, and ...se his own soul; *For he that ...ll gain the world, with the loss ...his soul, will be a great loser in the* ...

...Beloved, That I have printed ...ose Sermons something larger ...an I preached them, by adding ...me small Editions to them, I ...cknowledge; and that which I ...ow desire of you, is, That
what

The Epistle

what you read in these Line[s]
you would practise in you[r]
Lives. O that you would op[en]
the door of your hearts to t[he]
Lord *Jesus*, (who stands knoc[k]-
ing at them) that he may come i[n]
and sup with you, and you with hi[m]
that you may be able to stand in t[he]
day of his wrath, when others w[ill]
cry to the Rocks and the Mounta[ins]
to fall on them. O Friends, G[od]
hath spared you in this time [of]
Calamity, and will you n[ot]
serve him? O! you have be[en]
as brands pluckt out of t[he]
burning: O therefore, humble your selves under Go[ds]
mighty hand, that you may [be]
exalted in due time. Wo[rk]
therefore, while it is called [to]
day; for the night cometh,
whi[ch]

Dedicatory.

which no man can work. Now Brethren, I commend you to God, and to the word of his Grace, which is able to build you up, and to give you an Inheritance among all them which are sanctified. I shall add no more, but promise you my prayers; and desiring yours also, That this may bring glory to God, and good to you; which is the desire of him, who is

Your Friend and Servant in the precious Concernments of the GOSPEL,

WILLIAM DYER.

THE
EPISTLE
TO THE
READER.

Courteous Reader,

I Have had little encouragement from the World, to appear any more in this nature, who have so many Books taken and kept from me, without any just Cause, though there was nothing in them, but it was profitable matter for the Church of God; yet for all this, they are kept from me still. But Reader, this is not all which I have suffered; for, as soon as my Books came forth, several Men made

The Epistle

made a prize of them, by Printi[ng]
them over divers times without [my]
knowledge, with many gross m[i]
stakes and abuses, which was not [a]
little trouble to me, to see how t[he]
Author and the Buyer were b[oth]
abused. Therefore Courteous R[ea]
der, this may give thee to und[er]
stand, That if thou hast occa[sion]
for any of my Books, thou ma[y]
have them at the Black-spre[ad]
Eagle, at the West end of Pau[ls]
truly Printed. Kind Reader [I]
hope these Sermons will find as [good]
acceptance with thee, as the [for]
mer; I confess, this encouraged [me]
when I considered how my for[mer]
Treatises were received and emb[ra]
ced by the Lords People in all [parts]
of this Kingdom, as appears b[y]
many thousands of them which [

Dedicatory.

Printed and sold; and though I
met with many discouragements
them without, and some also
are within, who have bent their
like a Bow, for lyes, as if I
done that which was never in my
ghts, nor in my heart, much less
ractise; and though they had as
cause to report it of me, as of
man; yet how confidently did some
, and others believe those abo-
able Lyes, as if I had lost my
Love, and were returning again
Egypt. O what is it that prejudice
malice will not do? But why
uld I be troubled at this, seeing it
so with the holy Apostle, who
through evil report, as well as
? But in this I rejoice, that the
d hath made me any way instru-
ntal in doing good, and in that he
hath

The Epistle, &c.

hath kept me close to himself; a[nd]
this is my Crown and rejoycing. No[w]
that the only wise God may keep th[ee]
and me by his Power, through Fai[th]
unto Salvation, that we may glori[fy]
him here, and reign with him herea[f-]
ter, is the desire and prayer of h[im]
who desires the good of thy soul,

WILLIAM DYER.

A Call to SINNERS;
OR,
Christ's Voice to London.

Revel. 3. 20.

Behold, I stand at the door and knock, if any man hear my voice, and open the door, I will come in to him, and will sup with him, and he with me.

THE holy Scriptures are the Mysteries of God, Christ is the Mysterie of the Scriptures, Grace is the Mysterie [of] Christ, 1 *Tim.* 3. 16. The Lord Jesus [is] our life, and the way to life, 1 *Cor.* 2. To know him savingly, believingly, experimentally, is life eternal, *John* [1]3. I am the way, saith Christ, *John* [1]6.

The old and good way, *Jer.* 6. 16.

The new and living way, *Heb.* 10.
The strait and narrow way, *Mat.* 7.
And because poor sinners are by [na]ture the children of wrath, and all g[one] out of the way, having their understa[nd]ings darkned, being alienated from [the] life of God, through the ignorance t[hat] is in them, because of the blindness [of] their hearts, *Ephes.* 4. 18. are beco[me] wretched, and miserable, and poor, [and] blind, and naked, like to the *Laodice[ans]* spoken of in this Chapter, *v.* 17.

Therefore the Lord Jesus, who is [full] of Love, full of Grace, and full of pit[y to] poor, lost sinners, doth graciously in[vite] them to come to him, that he may en[rich] them with his Gold, clothe them [with] his white raiment, and anoint their e[yes] with his eye-salve, that they may se[e, v.] 18. and further, to shew his willingne[ss and] readiness to save souls, he tells us in [the] text, *That he stands at the door and kno[cks,] that if any man hears his voice, and op[ens] the door, he will come in to him, and [will] sup with him, and he with me.*

these words you have three general...

1. Gods gracious offer to man; *Behold, I stand at the door and knock.*

2. Mans duty in relation to Gods gracious offer, *If any man hear my voice, open the door.*

3dly, God's gracious promise in relation to mans duty, *I will come in to him, I will sup with him, and he with me.*

The words being thus opened, there [arise] from them these four points of doctrine:

Doct. 1. *That there is a marvellous willingness in the heart of God and Christ to save and receive poor sinners.*

Doct. 2. *That the hearts of poor sinners are barred and bolted against the Lord Jesus.*

Doct. 3. *That it is the duty and great concernment of all men whatever, to hear Gods Voice, and to open the door.*

Doct. 4. *That whoever will but hear Christs voice, and open the door, he will come in*

to them, and sup with them, and [with him]
with him.

Neither time nor strength, belo[w]
will give me leave to handle all t[he]
Doctrines apart, therefore I shall i[nsist]
but upon one of them, which is th[e se]-
cond, *That the hearts of poor sinners* [are]
barr'd and bolted against the Lord [Je]-
sus.

In the prosecution of this point I [shall]
do three things:
1. Open it, that you may see it.
2. Prove it, that you may belie[ve it.]
3*dly*, Apply it, that you may rec[eive]
it.

First, In the opening of it, there [are]
three things to be explained.
1. The Bars.
2. The Voices.
3. The Doors.

1. I shall shew you what the Bars [are]
that bolts the door of our hearts ag[ainst]
Christ.

Beloved, they are six.
1. There is the Bar of Ignoranc[e.]
2.

2. The Bar of Unbelief.
3. The Bar of self-conceitedness.
4. The Bar of Earthly-mindedness.
5. The Bar of Prejudice.
6. The Bar of hardness of heart.

These (my Beloved) are the cursed bars, which bars God, and Christ, and the holy Spirit out of our hearts.

I shall begin first with the Bar of Ignorance, and in that I shall shew you three things:

First, What Ignorance is.

Secondly, What sinners are ignorant of.

Thirdly, The mischievousness of this sin of ignorance.

And, First, What ignorance is: Ignorance is the want of knowledge, or darkness of the understanding, for so saith the Apostle *Paul*, Eph. 4. 18. *Having the understanding darkned, being alienated from the life of God, through the ignorance that is in them, because of the blindness of their heart.* Here you may see

see what ignorance is, the Apostle [calls]
it darkness and blindness: So likewi[se]
2 *Cor.* 4. 3, 4. *But if our Gospel be hid,* [it is]
hid to them that are lost, in whom the [god]
of this world hath blinded the mind [of]
them which believe not, lest the light o[f the]
glorious Gospel of Christ, who is the I[mage]
of God, should shine unto them. So tha[t ig]-
norance is darkness of mind, blindne[ss of]
heart, and want of knowledge and s[piri]-
tual understanding in the soul.

Secondly, What are sinners igno[rant]
of?

Ans. 1. They are ignorant of G[od,]
they are ignorant of Christ, they are [ig]-
norant of the Spirit, they are igno[rant]
of the Word, they are ignorant of t[heir]
own misery; they are ignorant of [the]
necessity of a change, of being bor[n a]-
gain, of being new Creatures, of be[ing]
converted and turned from darkness [to]
light, from death to life, and from [the]
power of Satan to the living God; s[uch]
things as these, I say they are ignorant [of,]
and this is that which keeps poor so[uls]
from going to Christ. O beloved!

many of those amongst us, who are ignorant. It was said of the Priests sons of *Eli*, that they were sons of *Belial*, and knew not the Lord, 1 *Sam*. 2. So in the Prophesie of *Jeremiah*, chap. 2. ver. 8. it is said, *The Priests said not, Where is the Lord? and they that handle the Law, know me not,* So the Pharisees were blind leaders of the blind, *Mat.* 15.14. Would to God there were no such among our Priests this day: May not that charge be drawn up against us now, as was against *Israel?* Hos. 4. 1. *Because there is no truth, nor mercy, nor knowledge of God in the Land; by swearing, and lying, and killing, and stealing, and committing Adultery, they break out, and blood toucheth blood, therefore the Land mourneth; and my people are destroyed for lack of knowledge: Because thou hast rejected knowledge, I will also reject thee, that thou shalt be no Priest to me, seeing thou hast forgotten the Law of thy God, I will also forget thy Children; they eat up the sins of my people, and set their hearts on their iniquity, and they are like people like Priest.* Thus

B 4

men

men err not knowing the Scriptures nor t[he] Power of God, Matt. 22. 29.

Thirdly, The mischievousness of t[he] sin of ignorance.

1. Ignorance is that which keeps m[e] from knowing of God.

2. Ignorance is that which keeps m[e] from pleasing of God.

3. Ignorance is that which keeps m[e] from coming to God.

4. Ignorance hinders men from h[a]ving a propriety in God.

5. Ignorance is that which harde[ns] the heart against God. O cursed a[nd] mischievous Ignorance! What sin li[ke] unto this? This is that which darke[ns] which hardens, which blinds and bars t[he] door of our hearts against Christ. *that thou hadst known* (said our dear Lor[d] *the things that belong to thy peace,* Lu[ke] 19. 42. *But because they are a people of [no] understanding, therefore he that ma[de] them, will have no mercy on them, and [he] that formed them, will shew them no f[a]vour,* Isa. 27. 11. Thus (my Beloved) [I] have shewed you what a wretched a[nd] mise[

[mi]serable state such are in that are thus [ig]norant.

[2]*dly*, The second Bar is Unbelief, [wh]ich barrs and bolts Christs out of our [h]earts; this is that which makes men,

1. That they give no credit to the re[por]t of the Gospel.

2. Neither do they yeild that loving [and] loyal subjection to Christ as their [Lo]rd, where unbelief is.

3. Where Unbelief is, it keeps off [the] heart from confidently depending [up]on Christ for that which is to be had [in] him, and so keeps Christ out of our [sou]ls; it is that which clips the wings of [his] mercy, *Heb.* 3. *ult.* it is that which [hol]ds the hand of his power, *Matt.* 13. *And he did not many mighty works [the]re, because of their unbelief.* It is that [wh]ich lets the soul into perdition, *John* [3.1]4. *Rev.* 21. 7. The unbelieving shall [hav]e their portion in the Lake of fire, [wh]ich is the second death. Unbelief is [tha]t which hardens the heart, and causes [to] depart from God; *Heb.* 3. 12. *Take [hee]d Brethren, lest there be in any of you*

an

an evil heart of unbelief, in departi[ng] from the living God; but exhort one a[no]ther daily, while it is called to day, left [any] of you be hardened. O Beloved, unbelief [is] that also, which gives God the lye; [he] that believeth not God, hath made hi[m] a lyar, because he believeth not the R[e]cord that God gave of his Son, 1 J[ohn] 5.10. They believe not his promi[ses,] fear not his threatnings, nor hea[r]ken [to] the voice of his Word; though he [sets] life and death before them, Heaven a[nd] Hell, bitter and sweet, yet they go on [in] the imagination of their heart, to a[dd] sin to sin, putting the evil day far aw[ay,] but draw iniquity with cords of van[ity] and sin (as it were) with a Cart Rope[:] beloved, this is the state and condi[tion] of unbelievers, and this is one of [the] bars that bolts Christ out of the hea[rt:] as all believers are in a state of salva[tion] so all unbelievers are in a state of d[am]nation; for, *He that believeth not, is* [con]*demned already*, John 3.18.

 3*dly*, The third Bar is self-con[ceit]edness, which bars and bolts the L[ord] J[esus]

Jesus out of the heart.

First, A Self-conceited man is one which supposes himself to be that he is not, *Gal.* 6. 3. *If a man think himself be somthing, when he is nothing, he deceiveth himself.*

Secondly, A self-conceited man is one that glorieth in his works, and despiseth others. *Luke* 18. 9, 10. *And he spake this parable unto certain which trusted in themselves, that they were righteous, and despised others. The Pharisee stood and prayed thus with himself: God I thank thee, that I am not as other men are; extortioners, Unjust, Adulterers, or even as this Publican.* But the Publican whom he dispised, went away rather justified: for every one that exalteth himself, shall be abased.

Thirdly, A Self-conceited man is the furthest from heaven of any man, *Verily I say unto you, that Publicans and Harlots go into the Kingdom of heaven before you,* saith our Saviour to the self-conceited Pharisees, *Mat.* 21. 31.

Fourthly,

Fourthly, a Self-conceited man is [he]
that liveth the most securest in a state [of]
sin and misery, *And it shall come to pa[ss]
when he heareth the words of this cur[se]
that he shall bless himself in his hea[rt]
saying, I shall have peace though I w[alk]
in the imagination of mine heart, to a[dd]
drunkenness unto thirst*, Deut. 29. 19.

Fifthly, A Self-conceited man is [the]
hardest to be wrought upon, and co[n]-
victed of the State and condition that [he]
is in, of any man; because he thin[ks]
himself righteous and holy enough, a[nd]
good and sound enough: thus it w[as]
with the Scribes and Pharisees who h[ad]
such high thoughts of themselves, t[hat]
they thought themselves to be the m[ost]
holiest persons in the world: mark w[hat]
Christ saith to them, *John*. 9. 12. T[he]
*whole need not a Physician; but they t[hat]
are sick; I came not to call the Righte[ous]
but sinners to Repentance*: so also it [is]
said *John* 7. 48. *Have any of the Ru[lers]
or of the Pharisees believed on him?* No[w]
these were very hard to be convi[ct]
and brought to own the truth.

Six[thly]

Sixthly, A Self-conceited man, is one that thinks that God is made up of nothing but mercy, and therefore he lives in his sins, and pleaseth himself with this, that God is merciful, he lying still in the ditch of sin, and crying God help, but never endeavoureth to come out; though the Lord waiteth to be gracious, yet the Lord is a God of Judgment, *Esa.* 30. 18. O! this is the sad and miserable condition of a Self-conceited man: This is that which keeps him from closeing with Christ, this is that cursed Bar, that bolts the door of our hearts against Christ.

The fourth Bar is Earthly-mindedness.

First, an Earthly-minded man, is one that minds the things of this world, more then he doth Jesus Christ; this was the Case of that young man in the Gospel, which came to Christ, and asked him saying, What good thing shall I do, to inherit eternal life? Jesus bids him keep the Commandements; he saith unto him, *All these have I kept from my youth*

youth up, what lack I yet: Jesus sai[d] unto him; if thou wilt be perfect, [sell] that thou hast, and give to the poor, a[nd] thou shalt have treasure in heaven: b[ut] he being an earthly minded man, wou[ld] not imbrace the Counsel of Christ, b[ut] went away sorrowful, for he had great p[os]sessions, *Mat.* 19. 21, 22.

Secondly, An Earthly-minded ma[n] is one that will leave the work of Go[d] to imbrace the present world; this w[as] *Pauls* complaint of *Demas,* 2 *Tim.* 4.[10] *For Demas hath forsaken me, havi[ng] loved this present world;* so also in *Ph[il.]* 2. 21. he saith, *that all seek their ow[n] not the things that are Jesus Christs.*

Thirdly, An Earthly minded man, [is] one that will preach false Doctrine, f[or] the love of money and filthy lucres sak[e] 1 *Tim.* 6. 10. *For the love of money* [is] *the root of all evil; which while so[me] have coveted after, they have err[ed] from the faith,* Tit. 1. 10, 11. *For the[re] are many unruly and vain talkers, a[nd] deceivers, which teach things they oug[ht] not, for filthy lucres sake,* 2 *Pet.* 2. 1[.]
whi[ch]

which have forsaken the right way, and are gone astray, following the way of Balaam the son of Bosor, who loved the wages of unrighteousness. O beloved! I could wish that this were not too much practised in this our day; but alas, what shall I say? Such is the Earthly mindedness of many of the Priests now, that I may say of them as the blessed Apostle *Paul*, said of the same in his day, *Phil.* 3. 19. *whose end is destruction, whose God is their belly, and whose glory is in their shame; who mind Earthly things.*

Fourthly, An Earthly minded man, is one that trusteth in his riches, and not in God; *Prov.* 11. 28. *He that trusteth in his riches shall fall*, *Psal.* 49. 6. *They that trust in their wealth, and boast themselves in the multitude of their riches, none of them can by any means redeem his brother, nor give to God a ransom for him;* therefore, *if riches do increase, set not your heart upon them*, *Psal.* 62. 11. The blessed Apostle *Paul*, doth charge them that be rich in this world, that they trust not in uncertain riches, but in the living God:

God, *Who giveth us richly all thing[s] [to] injoy,* 1 *Tim.* 6. 17. Thus you may see beloved, that whoever trusteth in [un]certain riches more then in God, is [an] earthly minded man; it is that wh[ich] bars men out of the Kingdom of heav[en;] it is the words of Christ to his Discip[les] *Mark* 10. 24, 25. *How hard is it [for] them that trust in riches, to enter into [the] Kingdom of God: It is easier for a Ca[mel] to go thorough the eye of a needle, then [for] a rich man to enter into the Kingdom [of] God.* O beloved! it is a snare, it is I[do]latry, *Col.* 3. 5. *And covetousness, wh[ich] is Idolatry, it is the root of all evil,* 1 T[im.] 6. 10. *For the love of money is the r[oot] of all evil;* thus Earthly mindedness, [or] covetousness is another great sin, t[hat] keeps souls from going to Christ for [life] and salvation. *And they all with one c[on]sent began to make excuse: The first s[aid] unto him, I have bought a piece of grou[nd] and I must needs go and see it, I pray [thee] have me excused: And another said, [I] have bought five yoke of Oxen, and I [go] to prove them, I pray thee have me exc[used]*

And another said, I have married a wife, and therefore I cannot come, Luk. 18, 19, 20.

The Fifth *Bar* is Prejudice, which bars Christ out of the heart: Wicked and sinful men have a great prejudice against Christ, that is, against these three things of Christ.

First, They have a prejudice against his Doctrine, or worship: *Many therefore of his Disciples when they heard this, said, this is an hard saying, who can bear it? from that time many of his Disciples went back, and walked no more with him:* John 6. 60. 66. *And they questioned among themselves saying, what thing is this? What new doctrine is this?* Mark 1. 27. Sinners, have a great prejudice against the doctrine and worship of Christ, they think it too pure, too spiritual, and too powerfull for them to bear.

Secondly, They have a great prejudice against the Ministers, (or Ambassadours) of Christ: they say of them as *Ahab* did of *Micajah, I hate him, for he never prophesies good of me:* 1 Kings 22. 8. so

C

8. so in 1 Kings 18. 17. Ahab [said] Elijah; Art thou he that troubleth Is[rael] so Jeremiah complains of this saying [I] am in derision daily; every one mock[eth] me, because the word of the Lord [was] made a reproach unto me, and a deri[sion] dayly, Jer. 20. 7. 8. So in the 24 of A[cts] ver. 5. it is said of Paul, for we h[ave] found this man a pestilent fellow, [and] a mover of sedition among all the J[ews] throughout the world, and a Ring-le[ad]er of the sect of the Nazarenes; [and] this is according to the words of [our] blessed Lord, Mat. 10. 22. And ye s[hall] be hated of all men for my name sake.

Thirdly, Sinners have a great pre[ju]dice against the members of Christ: [and] that for four Reasons.

1. Because they are poor Luke [6.] 22, 23. 1 Cor. 1 26, 27, 28, 29. 1 C[or.] 11. 22. Or despise ye the Church of Go[d] and shame them that are poor.

2. Because they are but a few, L[uke] 12. 32. Mat. 7. 14. Deut. 7. 7. for [ye] were the fewest of all people; Rev. 3[.] Thou hast a few names in Sardis, wh[ich] ha[ve]

...ve not defiled their Garments.

3. Because they are unlearned in the ...unt of men: this is said of Christ, ...17.15. *How knoweth this man letting, having never learned.* Also of *Peter* ...*John* it is said *Act.* 4. 13. *And when* ...*perceived that they were unlearned* ...*ignorant men, they marvelled, and* ...*took knowledg of them, that they had* ...*with Jesus. Are ye also deceived?* ...*ve any of the Rulers or of the Pharisees* ...*ved on him? But this people who* ...*eth not the Law, are cursed,* John 7. ...48.

4. Because they will not Conform to ...s Inventions, See 2 Chron. 11. 13, ...*And the Priests and the Levites that* ...*re in all Israel, resorted to Rehoboam out* ...*all their Coasts; for they left their suburbs* ...*their possessions, and came to Judah, and* ...*usalem; for Jereboam and his sons* ...*cast them off from executing the priests* ...*fice before the Lord, and after them* ...*of all the Tribes of Israel, such as set* ...*ir hearts to seek the Lord God of Israel,* ...*me to Jerusalem to sacrifice to the Lord*

C 2 God

God of their Fathers, ver. 16. See D[an.]
3. 18. *Be it known unto thee, O King, [that]
we will not serve thy Gods, nor worship [the]
Golden Image that thou hast set up.* A[lso]
in Matt. 15. 2. *Why do thy Disciples tra[ns]-
gress the tradition of the Elders, for t[hey]
wash not their hands when they eat bre[ad.]
But Jesus said unto them, Why do ye [also]
transgress the Commandment of God [by]
your tradition.* See also Acts 5. 28, [29.
Did not we straitly command you, that [ye]
should teach no more in this Name, and [be-]
hold ye have filled Ierusalem with your [Do-]
ctrine, and intend to bring this mans bl[ood]
upon us: Then Peter and the other A[po-]
stles answered and said, We ought to [obey]
God rather than men.* See Col. 2. 21, [22.
Touch not, tast not, handle not, which [all]
are to perish with the using, after the Co[m-]
mandments and Doctrines of men.* [O]
my dear Brethren, this cursed sin of P[re-]
judice is that which keeps sinners fr[om]
receiving the Truth in the love of it, [and]
a bar which bolts Christ out of [the]

The sixth Barr is hardness of heart, which bolts the heart of sinners against Christ; and they are hardned,

1. Against God, *Iob* 9. 4. *Who hath hardned himself against him, and hath prospered?*

2. Their hearts are hardned against mercy, that it doth not draw them, *Rom.* 2.4,5. *Or despisest thou the riches of his goodness, and forbearance, and long-suffering, not knowing that the goodness of God leadeth thee to repentance; but after thy hardness and impenitent heart, treasurest up unto thy self wrath against the day of wrath, and revelation of the righteous judgement of God.*

3. Their hearts are hardned against his Judgements, that they do not tremble at them, as it is said *Exod.* 8.32. *And Pharoah hardned his heart at this time also, neither would he let the people go;* As it is also said, *Ier.* 5. 22. *Fear ye not me, saith the Lord, and will ye not tremble at my presence?*

4. Their hearts are hardned against his word, that it doth not reform them,

C 3 Prov.

Prov. 29. 1. *He that being often reprove[d]* *hardneth his neck, shall suddenly be destro[y]ed, and that without remedy*, *seeing th[ou] hatest instruction, and castest my word b[ehind] bind thee*, Psal. 50. See in Jer. 44. 16. [*As] for the word which thou hast spoken to us [in] the Name of the Lord, we will not hearke[n] to thee, but we will certainly do whatsoev[er] cometh out of our own mouth.*

5. Their hearts are hardned again[st] the Spirit of God, that it doth not m[ove] them, Gen. 6. 3. *My spirit shall not alw[ayes] strive with man*: As Stephen said to t[he] Jews, Acts 7. 51. *Ye stiff-necked and u[n]circumcised in hearts and ears, ye do alw[ayes] resist the holy Ghost; as your fathers di[d, so] do ye.*

6. Their hearts are hardned agai[nst] all the means of Grace, or gracious i[n]vitations from the people of God; B[ut] *they refused to hearken, and pulled a[way] the shoulder, and stopped the ear, and ma[de] the heart like an Adamant stone, lest th[ey] should hear the Law, and the words whi[ch] the Lord of Hosts sent to them by his [spi]rit in the former Prophets.* Zech. 7. 11, [12.]

they are like the deaf *Adder that stoppeth* *her* *ear, which will not hearken to the voice* *of Charmers, charming never so wisely,* Psal. 58. 4, 5. O dear Friends, this is another Bar which bolts Christ out of the hearts of poor sinners: Thus Beloved, I have shewed you what the Barrs are that bolts the door of our hearts against Christ, that we do not hear his voice, and open the door.

Secondly, The second thing which is here to be explained, is, what this voice which sinners are to hear, it is the Voice of Christ, he is speaking to poor sinners to open the door of their hearts, that he may come in and sup with them. There are two sorts of Voices by which Christ speaketh to the soul, Inward Voices, and outward Voices.

First, Inward Voices.

1. The Voice of Conscience; The Lord Jesus speaks to sinners by their Consciences; it is said of the Jews, *Joh.* 9. They were convicted by their own Consciences; so *Paul* saith in Rom. 9. 1, *my Conscience beareth me witness*: And

of the Gentiles *Paul* saith, *Rom.* 2.1[?] that they did by nature the things co[n]tained in the Law, their Consciences [al]so bearing them witness; and as *P[aul]* saith 2 *Cor.* 1.12. *Our rejoicing is this,[the] testimony of our Conscience.* O Frien[ds] God preacheth to you many times [by] your Consciences, which speaketh [to] you secretly and powerfully, condem[n]ing and reproving you for your iniq[ui]ties; O therefore hear the Voice of Co[n]science, for it is the voice of Christ, he[ar] (I say) and hearken to it, and let Ch[rist] in, that he may sup with you.

2. Christ speaks to us by the voice [of] his Spirit, as he did to the old wor[ld] *Gen.* 6.3. *My Spirit shall not always stri[ve] with man;* and as he did to the Jews, A[cts] 7.51. *Ye do always resist the holy Gh[ost] as your fathers did, so do ye;* so in *Iohn* 1[6.] 8. Christ tells us, that the Spirit shou[ld] *convince the world of sin, of righteo[us]ness, and of judgement.* O! the e[ver] blessed God speaks to the world by [his] blessed Spirit, striving with them, co[n]vincing of them, and reproving th[em]

for their iniquities, that their souls may believe in him, and live with him to all eternity.

Secondly, There are outward voices by which Christ speaks to sinners.

1. By the voice of his Word, which is the preaching of the Gospel, that is the word of reconciliation: O sinner, when thou hearest the word read, thou hearest the voice of Christ, Col. 1. 5. *Whereof ye heard before in the word of the truth of the Gospel*; as Christ saith, John 5.39. *Search the Scriptures, for they are they that testifie of me*: the voice of the Scriptures is the voice of Christ, and as Christ speaks to us by them here, so he will judge us by them hereafter, Rom. 2. 16. *God will judge the secrets of men by Christ Iesus, according to my Gospel*; Joh. 12. *ult.* where Christ saith, *The Word which I have spoken, the same shall judge him in the last day.*

2. Christ speaks to sinners by the voice of his Rod, by afflictions and tribulations, and judgments, Mich. 6.9. *The Lords voice cryeth unto the City, and the*

man

man of wisdom shall see thy Name; hear ye the Rod, and who hath appointed it.

3. Christ speaks to sinners by the voice of his servants, as in Isa.50.10, *Who is there among you that feareth the Lord, that obeyeth the voice of his servant.* So in 2 Cor.5.20. *Now then we are Embassadors for Christ, as though God did beseech you by us, we pray you in Christs stead, be ye reconciled to God:* So in Matth. 10. *He that heareth you, heareth me.* O sinners! Christ speaks to you by the voice of his servants, by his Ministers and Members, who beseech you, and entreat you to be reconciled, that you may have peace with God through Jesus Christ.

Having thus briefly shewed you what the Voices are:

Thirdly, I shall in the third place come to shew you, What the Door is that Christ stands and knocks at, which sinners are to open and let him in.

1. The first Door which sinners should open unto Christ, is the door of their thoughts; I say, we must open the door of our thoughts to him, that God may
be

in our thoughts, and Christ in our thoughts, and the Spirit of Life and power in our thoughts, and Eternity in our thoughts, Heaven and Judgement in our thoughts: *Keep this for ever in the imagination of the thoughts of thy heart*, 1 Chron. 29.18. *How precious also are thy thoughts unto me, O God, how great is the sum of them!* Psal. 139.17. *In the multitude of my thoughts within me, thy comforts delight my soul*, Psal. 94. 19. O! this is the first door of our hearts which believers open to their beloved Lord.

2*dly*, The second is the door of Consideration which sinners should open to Christ: O that they were wise, and understood this, *that they would consider their latter end*, Deut. 32.29. *The Oxe knoweth his owner, and the Ass his Masters Crib, but Israel doth not know, my people doth not consider*, Isa. 1.3. *The Tabret, and Pipe, and Harp, and Wine are in their Feasts, but they regard not the work of the Lord, neither consider the operation of his hands*, Isa. 5.12. But now those that have

have opened this door to Christ, the consider their ways. *The upright consider eth his ways,* Prov.21.29. *and the wondrous works of God,* Job 37.14. *and what great things God hath done for him,* 1 Sam. 12.24. *Therefore thus saith the Lord of Hosts, consider your ways,* Hag.1.5. And this is the second door of the heart.

3*dly*, The third door is the door of affection, which sinners should open to Christ: *Thou shalt love the Lord thy God with all thy heart, and with all thy soul,* Deut.6.5. *If any man love not the Lord Iesus, let him be anathema maranatha,* 1 Cor.16.22. *Grace be with all them that love our Lord Iesus Christ in truth & sincerity,* Eph.6.24. *Set your affections on things above, and not on things beneath,* Col.3.1. this door of love and affection must be opened to Christ, that he may come in to your hearts, and be your nearest and dearest, your joy and delight, that you may have reconciliation with the Father, union with the Son, and communion with the Holy Ghost: And this is the third door of the heart.

4*thly*,

4thly, The fourth is the door of Desire, which must be opened to Christ, or else he cannot come in to our hearts, and sup with us. O sinners, you must desire and thirst after Christ vehemently, and say as the Church doth in the last of *Canticles, ult. Make hast my Beloved, and be thou like to a Roe, or to a young Hart upon the Mountains of Spices:* So in Rev. 22.20. *Even so come Lord Iesus, come quickly.* So with the Psalmist, Psal. 73. 25. *Whom have I in Heaven but thee, and there is none on earth to be desired besides thee.* And with the Church, Isa. 26. *With my soul have I desired thee in the night, yea, with my Spirit within me will I seek thee early, for the desire of my soul is to thy Name, and to the remembrance of thee.* So with *Paul, I desire to know nothing among you, save Iesus Christ, and him crucified,* 1 Cor. 2.2. This is the fourth door of the heart which you must open to Christ, without which there is no supping with Christ, nor Christ with you.

5thly,

5thly, The fifth is the door of Estimation, which sinners must open to Christ, that is, to prise him, and to value him as more precious then all other things besides; so do believers, 1 Pete. 2.7. *Unto you therefore which believe, he is precious*; and with Paul, *do count all things but dung and dirt to gain him*; and also with *Moses, to esteem the reproach of Christ greater riches then the Treasures of Egypt*, Heb. 11.25. O! those blessed souls that have opened this door to Christ, he is to them all lovely, the chiefest among ten thousands; yea, he is better than Rubies, and all the things thou canst desire, are not to be compared unto him, *Prov.* 3.15. so it must be with you, poor souls, you must look upon Christ as most lovely, most precious, most desirable, and most glorious; thus he is to the Father, to the holy Angels, and to the Saints. And this is the fifth door of the heart.

6thly, The sixt is the door of a good Conversation, which sinners as well as Saints

Saints must open to Christ: *For our conversation is in Heaven, from whence also we look for a Saviour, the Lord Iesus,* Phil. 3.20. *For the Grace of God that bringeth salvation, hath appeared to all men, and teacheth us, that denying ungodliness and worldly lusts, we should live soberly, and godly, and righteously in this present world.* Tit. 3.11. *Seeing then that all these things shall be dissolved, what manner of persons ought ye to be in all holy conversation and godliness,* 2 Pet. 3.11. *Only let your conversation be as becometh the Gospel of Christ,* Phil. 1.29. *And to him that ordereth his conversation aright, will I shew the salvation of God.* This is the sixt door of the heart, to wit, a good Conversation; this also must be opened to Christ, that he may come in, and sup with us, and we with him, that our souls may have fellowship and Communion with him. And thus I have briefly shewed you, beloved, what the Doors are that must be opened to Christ: Now having done with the Explanation, I come to the Application of the point,

and

and as I have opened it to you, that yo[u]
might see it, and proved it to you, th[at]
you might believe it, I shall now app[ly]
it, that you may receive it.

Is it so, beloved, that the hearts [of]
sinners are thus barr'd and bolted a[-]
gainst the Lord Jesus?

Use 1. First by way of *Information*[.]
This may be of use to inform us of th[e]
sad and miserable condition of all un[-]
converted persons; they are wretche[d]
and miserable, and poor, and blind, an[d]
naked; they are without Christ, bein[g]
aliens from the Commonwealth of I[s-]
rael, and strangers to the Covenant [of]
promise, having no hope, and witho[ut]
God in the world, *Eph.* 2.12. O sinner[s]
this is your condition, who are gracele[ss]
and Christless persons, and though th[is]
be sad, yet this is not all, for your hear[ts]
are barr'd and bolted against the Lor[d]
of Life and glory: O thou that hea[r-]
est or readest this, how canst thou b[ut]
tremble to think that thy heart shoul[d]

thus barr'd and bolted against Jesus Christ with Ignorance, with Unbelief, self-conceitedness, Earthly-mindedness, prejudice and hardness of heart; and yet all this while open to Sin, to Satan, and to the World, which are cruel Enemies to thy soul: That I may hasten you out of this condition, if it be the will of God, (as the Angel did *Lot* out of *Sodom, Gen.* 19.) I shall turn my Discourse into an Exhortation.

Use 2. And first of all, let me exhort you whose hearts are thus barr'd and bolted against Jesus Christ, to hear his Voice, and to open the door.

1. To hear his Voice; O sinners, Christ speaks to you by your Consciences, by his Spirit, by his Word, by his Rod, and by his Servants: O you Men and women of this City, God hath spoken to you by all these Voices, but you have turned the deaf ear to Christ. *The Voice of the Lord cryeth to the City, (and the man of wisdom shall see thy Name) hear ye the Rod, and who hath ap-*

D *pointed*

pointed it, Micha 6. 9. O *London, London*! God speaks to thee by his Judgments, and because thou wouldst n[ot] hear the Voice of his Word, he ha[th] made thee to feel the stroke of his Ro[d] O great City! how hath the Plag[ue] broke in upon thee, because of [all] thy abominations? *Thus they provok[ed] him to anger with their inventions, a[nd] the Plague brake in upon them*, Psal. 10[6.] 29. O you of this City! how is t[he] wrath of the Lord kindled against yo[u,] that such multitudes of thousands a[re] fallen within thy borders by the noiso[me] Pestilence, God's immediate Sword? [O] *London*! how are thy Streets thinne[d,] thy Widows encreased, and thy buryi[ng] places filled, thy Inhabitants fled, t[hy] Trade decayed! O therefore lay [to] heart, you that are yet alive, all th[ese] things, and turn from your wick[ed] wayes, that the cry of your praye[rs] may outcry the cry of your sins, a[nd] be like unto the City of *Nineveh*, w[ho] believed God, and gave credit to *Jo[nah]* his words, who humbled themselv[es] and fasted, and cryed mightily unto the Lord, *Jonas* 3. 5. O let not Heathens outstrip Christians; Did *Niniveh* repent and turn from their wicked wayes, and shall not *London*? May be you may think (my Brethren) that all is well now, and that God is friends with you, because the sickness decreaseth and abateth; I say, blessed be God for it; but be not deceived, God is not mocked; to whomsoever God bestows great mercies, if they abound in great wickedness, he will inflict great punishments upon them. Alas beloved, do your sins decrease? And doth that abate? Is there a turning from sin, and a turning to God? Is there a Reformation and amendment of life amongst you? If this be so, then you may hope that God hath done afflicting of you: *If my people which are called by my Name, shall humble themselves, and pray, and seek my face, and turn from their wicked wayes, then will I forgive their sin, and heal their land,* 2 Chron. 7. 4. But if you remain still as prophane as before, as superstitious as before, as

D 2   carnal

carnal as before, as lukewarm as before, as hard-hearted and cruel as before, as proud & vain as before; I say, if it be thus with you, God hath not yet done with *London*, but hath other Judgements to pour out upon you, though he cause this to cease; do but see how God dealt with the *Jews* in this case, *Amos* 4.6. *I have given you cleaness of teeth in all your Cities, and want of bread in all your places, yet have you not returned unto me, saith the Lord. I have also with-holden the rain from you, yet have ye not returned unto me, saith the Lord; I have smitten you with blasting and mildew, yet have ye not returned unto me, saith the Lord. I have sent among you the Pestilence after the manner of Egypt, your young men have I slain with the Sword, and have taken away your horses, and I have made the stink of your Camps to come up into your nostrils, yet have ye not returned unto me, saith the Lord. I have overthrown some of you, as God overthrew Sodom and Gomorrah and ye were as a fire brand pluckt out of the burning, yet have ye not return-*

Chrifts Voice to London. 37

[un]to me, *faith the Lord. Therefore thus
[wi]ll I do unto thee, O Ifrael, and becaufe
[I w]ill do this unto thee; prepare to meet thy
[Go]d, O Ifrael.* Therefore my dear Bre-
[th]ren, for Gods fake, for Chrifts fake,
[an]d for your fouls fake, hear Chrifts
[V]oice, that you may be profperous on
[ear]th, and glorious in Heaven.

2. Let me exhort you, and O that I
[co]uld prevail with you to perfwade you
[of] this City to three things.

1. That you would throughly turn
[fr]om your evil ways, and amend your
[do]ings, that God may repent him of the
[evi]l which otherwife he may bring upon
[yo]u. O fee what the Lord faith, *Jer.*26
[8.] *If fo be they will hearken, and turn
[ev]ery man from his evil way, that I may
[re]pent me of the evil which I purpofe to do
[un]to them, becaufe of their doings,* fee ver.
[1]3. *Therefore now amend your wayes
[an]d your doings, and obey the voice of
[th]e Lord your God, and the Lord will
[re]pent him of the evil that he hath pur-
[po]fed againft you.* Alfo mark what
[th]e Lord fpeaketh by the Prophet, Jer.

D 3   7.3.

7. 3. *Thus saith the Lord of Hosts, the God of Israel, amend your ways and your doings, and I will cause you to dwell in this place,* Ver. 5. If ye throughly amend your ways aud your doings, O Beloved, the Lord our God is willing to heal, willing to hear, and willing to forgive. Great Cities are places which are usually guilty of great sins, great provocations, and great abominations, and for this cause hath God destroyed and overthrown many Cities, as the Cities of Sodom and *Gomorrah,* Gen. 19. 24. *Then the Lord rained upon Sodom and Gomorrah fire and brimstone from the Lord out of heaven.* Also *Admah* and *Zeboim,* Hos. 11. 8. *How shall I make thee as Admah and set thee as Zeboim:* So *Jerusalem* and other Cities were destroyed by God for their sins and wickedness, 2 Chron. 35. 19. *Jer.* 52. 13, 14. Now see what the Apostle *Peter* saith of this, 2 Pet. 2. 6. *And turning the Cities of Sodom and Gomorrah into ashes, condemned them with an overthrow, making them an ensample unto those that after should live ungodly*

O London, repent, that it may not be so with thee. O ye people! rent your hearts, and not your garments, and turn unto the Lord, who is willing to receive you, that so his Judgements may be diverted, your former Mercies restored, and his blessings poured down upon you.

2dly, That you would dearly love, and highly prize those precious Saints and Servants of the Most High God, which are amongst you. These are they of whom the world is not worthy, *Heb.* 11. 38. God prises them as his Jewels and Treasures, *Mal.* 3. 17. *Exod.* 19. 5. God calls them the dearly beloved of his soul, *Jer.* 12. 7. They are a chosen generation, a Royal Priesthood, an holy Nation, a peculiar people, 1 *Pet.* 2. 9. O therefore, he suffereth no man to do them wrong; yea, he reproves Kings for their sakes, *Psal.* 105. 14. O Beloved, Nations, and Cities, and Kings are blessed for their sakes, see *Gen.* 12. 2, 3. *And thou shalt be a blessing, I will bless them that bless thee, and curse him that curseth thee.* O *London*, in this thou art happy,

happy, yea more happy than any one City upon the face of the Earth (that I know, or have heard of) because thou hast within thy borders more righteous, more Saints, more true Believers, who are still sighing and mourning for thy sins, praying for thy peace, and seeking and desiring thy eternal good.

3*dly*, And lastly, let me exhort you to open the door, and let Christ in, into your Thoughts, into your Minds, into your Affections, into your Desires, into your Estimations, and into your Conversations. O Beloved, keep Christ out no longer, but let him into your hearts and souls, that he may make you rich, rich in Faith, rich in Knowledge, rich in Assurance, rich in Priviledges, rich in Experiences, and rich in good works. O therefore, let not sin be let in, and Christ shut out. O let Jesus Christ into your hearts, for if you shut the door against Christ, he will shut the door against you.

First, The door of Mercy.
Secondly, The door of Acceptance.
Thirdly, The door of Salvation.

First, The door of Mercy will be shut against you: Such whom Christ calls to, and they will not hear, they shall call, but Christ will not hear, *Prov.*1.24. *Because I have called, and ye have refused, I have stretched out my hand and no man regarded.* Ver.28. *Then shall they call upon me, but I will not answer, they shall seek me early, but they shall not find me; mine eye shall not spare, neither will I have pity; and though they cry in mine ears with a loud voice, yet will I not hear them,* Ezek. 8. 18. *Therefore thus saith the Lord, Behold, I will bring evil upon them, which they shall not be able to escape; and though they shall cry unto me, I will not hearken unto them,* Jer. 11. 1. *Because they have behaved themselves ill in their doings,* Mich. 3. 4. Thus my beloved, you see how the door of Gods Mercy will be shut against you, if you shut the door of your hearts against Christ.

Second-

2dly. The door of Acceptance will [be] shut against you, if you shut the door [of] your hearts against Christ; *Thus sai[th] the Lord unto this people, thus have th[ey] loved to wander, therefore the Lord do[th] not accept them: when they fast I w[ill] not hear their cry, and when they of[fer] burnt-Offerings and an Oblation I will n[ot] accept them.* Jer. 14. 10, 12. *To wh[at] purpose cometh there to me incense fro[m] Sheba? and sweet Cane from a far Coun[try]? your burnt offerings are not accepta[ble], nor your sacrifices sweet unto me,* Je[r.] 6. 20. *I hate, I despise your Feast-day[s] and I will not smell in your solemn assem[blies; and though ye offer me offerings, I will not accept them,* Amos. 5. 21,2[2.] O beloved, those that will not acce[pt] of Christ, shall not be accepted [in] Christ: *Who hath made us accepted [in] the Beloved,* Ephes. 1. 6.

3dly. The door of Salvation will be sh[ut] against you, if you shut the door of yo[ur] hearts against Christ. He that ma[de] you, will not save you, and he that fa[voured you, will shew you no favou[r] but as you have refused to open the dore of your hearts to our Saviour; so he will refuse to own you as his people, and open the door of Salvation for you; see the words of our blessed Lord himself, *Luk.* 13. 25. *When once the Master of the house is risen up and hath shut too the door and ye begin to stand without and to knock at the door, saying Lord, Lord, open unto us; and he shall answer and say unto you; I know you not, whence you are: depart from me all ye workers of iniquity. Then shall be weeping and gnashing of teeth, when ye shall see Abraham, Isaac and Jacob, and all the Prophets in the Kingdom of God, and ye your selves thrust out.* Consider what hath been said, And the Lord give you understanding in all things.

The end of the First Sermon.

THE
Great Day
Of His
WRATH

REVEL. **6. 17.**

in the great day of his Wrath is come, and who shall be able to stand!

Every mans thoughts runs now like *Nebuchadnezzars*, with a desire to know what shall come to pass hereafter, or what things ſme will bring forth, *Dan.* 2. 29. There nothing in the Womb of time, but
what

what was first in the womb of God,

Now this book of the *Revelat[ion]* shews us these three things.

1. The State and Condition of [the] true Church of Christ upon earth; [un]der the power and reign of Antich[rist.]

2. The rise, the reign, and rage [of] Antichrist in the World.

3. The quiet, blessed, and glori[ous] state and condition of the true Chu[rch] here below; after the ruine and do[wn]fall of Antichrist, the coming of Ch[rist] will be the ruine of Antichrist, 2 *Th[es.]* 2. 8, *Whom the Lord shall consume w[ith] the Spirit of his mouth, and shall dest[roy] with the brightness of his coming.* T[his] is decreed in heaven, and declared [on] earth.

This Chapter out of which my Te[xt] is taken, shews us seven things.

1. Here you may see what Go[d's] dreadful Judgments are; by which [he] cuts off, and destroys the Inhabita[nts] of the Earth, for their sin and wicke[d]ness: they are likened (or compare[d]) to Horses, as you may see from v[erse]

ver. 8. *Here you have a red horse, the* [sword]: *A black horse, the famine: A* [pale] *horse, the pestilence (or Plague) which* [leads] *to death.*

Horses are Creatures, which run to [and] fro, and so do Gods Judgments: [from] house, to house; from street, to [street]; from City, to city; from town, [to] town; and from one parish, to another; *And the Lord said, go ye after him* [through] *the City; and smite: let not* [your] *eye spare, neither have ye pity. Ezek.* [9]. so *Jer.* 5. 1,2,3,4,5 6.

Horses are Creatures, which are very [swift] in their motion, they run many [miles] in a little time: and therefore [men] ride them post. Gods Judgments [are] also very swift, they do much execution in a little time. So the Lord sent [a] pestilence upon *Israel*, from the morning, even to the time appointed: and [there] died of the people from *Dan*, even [to] *Beersheba*, seventy thousand men, [2] *Sam.* 24. 15. 2 *Chron.* 32. 21. You [may] also see a proof of this, by what [God] hath done to *London*, when there
fell

fell of the people above a thousand [a] day.

2. You may see here, where all t[he] Holy Martyrs and witnesses of Je[sus] Christ are, who have been slain for t[he] word of God, and for the Testimony [of] Jesus, they are under the Altar, v.6. Th[at] is, under the glorious protection [of] Christ in heaven. *They are before t[he] Throne of God, serving him day a[nd] night, and the Lamb leads them to t[he] living fountain, and God wipes aw[ay] all tears from their eyes.* Rev. 7. 15, 1[6,] 17.

3. You may see also the cause f[or] which these blessed souls were slain, [it] was for the word of God, and for t[he] Testimony of Jesus Christ. ver. 9.

4. Here you may see, that all t[he] Saints pretious blood which hath be[en] spilt from time to time, by the who[re] of *Babylon*, cryeth aloud day and nigh[t] to God for vengeance upon *Babyl*[on] ver. 10.

5. You have here the answer of Go[d] in relation to the Saints Cry, and [it] w[as]

said unto them, That they should rest for a little while, until their fellow servants also, and their brethren, that should [be] *killed as they were, should be fulfilled,* ver. 11.

6. You may here see what dreadfull and terrible things, followed upon the opening of the sixth Seal, ver. 12. *And there was a great Earth-quake; and the Sun became black as sack-cloth of hair, and the moon became as blood, and the* [stars] *of heaven fell unto the earth. And the heaven departed as a Scrole when it is rolled together; and every mountain and Island were moved out of their places.* These are the visible Judgments of God which are to come, upon the Antichristian Crew.

7. And lastly; this Chapter shews us, what will be the state and condition of those men at that day, who are found enemies to God and his people, ver. 15. *And the Kings of the Earth, and the great men, and the rich men, and the chief Captains, and the mighty men, and every bond-man, and every free-*

E

free-man, *hid themselves in the De[ns] and in the rocks of the mountains*, ve[rse] 16. *And said to the mountains and rock[s] fall on us, and hide us from the face [of] him that sitteth on the Throne, and fr[om] the wrath of the Lamb.*

Now this brings me to the words [of] my Text; which shews us the Reaso[n] of this great out-cry: *for the great d[ay] of his Wrath is come; and who shall be [a]ble to stand?*

The words of my Text contain tw[o] things: **A** Reason, and a Question.

1. The former part is the Groun[d] (or Reason) of this great out-cry her[e] made by the Kings, and great men [of] the earth, together with every bond[-]man and free-man; *for the great day [of] his wrath is come.*

2. The latter part is a Question pro[-]posed about standing at that day, *An[d] who shall be able to stand?*

The point of Doctrine which I sh[all] lay down from these words, is this,

Doct. *That the greatest part of Me[n] and Women will not be able to stand i[n] th[e]*

The Great Day of his Wrath.

Day of Gods Wrath.

In the handling of this point, I shall [shew] you four things.

1. That there are some days greater [than] others.

2. The nature and property of this [great] day.

3. And thirdly, Who they are, that [shall] not be able to stand in this day of [Gods] wrath.

4. The *Use* and *Application*.

In the first place, I shall shew you, [Beloved], that there are some great Days [spoken] of in the Scripture; See *Jer.* 30. [7.] *Alas! for that day is great, so that [none] is like it: It is even the time of Ja-[cobs] troubles, but he shall be saved out of [it.]*

The second great day you have in [Hosea] 1.11. *Then shall the Children of [Judah], and the Children of Israel be ga-[there]d together, and appoint themselves one [hea]d; and they shall come up out of the land, [for] great shall be the day of Jezreel.*

E 2   The

The third great day you have in [Joel] 2. 31. *The sun shall be turned into d[ark]ness, and the moon into blood, before [the] great and terrible day of the Lord come[th].*

The fourth great day you have [in] *Mal. 4. 5. Behold I will send you El[ijah] the Prophet, before the coming of [the] great and dreadfull day of the Lord.*

The fifth great day is this in my T[ext.] *For the great day of his wrath is come, [and] who shall be able to stand?*

The sixth great day, you have [in] *Rev. 16. 14. For they are the Spirit[s of] devils working miracles, which go f[orth] unto the Kings of the earth, and of [the] whole world, to gather them to the b[attle] of that great day of God Almighty.*

The seventh and last great day [you] have in the Epistle of *Jude*, ver. 6. [*And*] *the Angels which kept not their first E*[*state*,] *but left their own habitation, he hath [re]served in everlasting Chains under d[ark]ness, unto the Judgment of the g[reat] Day.* Thus beloved you see that th[ere] are some days greater then oth[ers,] which the Scripture calls great days,

Chriſts Voice to London. 53

[...]e of the greatneſs of the work which [Go]d doth, and will do: in thoſe [day]s.

[...], I ſhall now ſhew you, the nature [and] property of this great day in my [tex]t, Which is called, The great day [of] Gods wrath.

[...]O my Brethren, this will be a very [drea]dfull and terrible day to the wicked, [who] call evil good, and good evil; who [put] darkneſs for light, and light for [dark]neſs; and put far from them the e-[vil] day, which is now haſtening upon [the]m.

[...] Firſt of all, this day, will be a day of [aſt]oniſhment to the wicked and ungod-[ly,] as it ſaid. Deut. 28. 28. *The Lord ſhall [ſmi]te them with madneſs and blindneſs and [aſto]niſhment of heart.* O, it will be with the [wic]ked as it was with *Nebuchadnezzar*, [Dan.] 3. 24. who was aſtoniſhed to be-[hol]d the works and wonders of God [whi]ch the Lord wrought for the delive-[ran]ce of thoſe which put their truſt in [him.] *Then Nebuchadnezzar the King [wa]s aſtonied, and roſe up in haſt, and ſpake,*

E 3 *and*

and said unto his Counsellors, Did no[t]
cast three men bound into the midst of [the]
fire? They answered and said unto the K[ing]
True, O King. He answered and said,
I see four men loose, walking in the m[idst]
of the fire, and they have no hurt, and [the]
form of the fourth is like the Son of G[od]
O Sinners! do but see here how
proud *Nebuchadnezzar* was astoni[shed]
at the beholding of this sight; here
three things that did astonish this g[reat]
King;

First, To see the fire, whose nat[ure]
is to burn and consume, to have
power to seize upon the bodies of t[hese]
men: Fire, is one of the cruellest c[rea]tures; it is a merciless creature, a[nd]
therefore the torments of hell is set fo[rth]
by fire, Mat. 25. 41. *Go ye cursed [into]
everlasting fire, prepared for the D[evil]
and his Angels.*

Secondly, The second thing which
astonish *Nebuchadnezzar*, was, to
the servants of the Lord, walk in
fiery furnace: *Did not we cast three [men]
bound into the midst of the fire? Lo I*

The great Day of his Wrath. 55

men loose, walking in the midst of the
...; They were cast in bound, but
now they are loose. Now that the fire
...uld have power on their bands, and
...on their bodies, O! this caused astonishment in *Nebuchadnezzar*.

Thirdly, The third thing that did a-
...nish him, was to see their number not
...creased, but increased: *Did not we
...t three men bound into the fire? and
I see four men walking in the midst of
...fire, and the form of the fourth, is
...e unto the Son of God.* And this did al-
...astonish this great King: Now as it
...as with *Nebuchadnezzar* here, so it will
...with the wicked in this great day. O
...ou that now speak proudly, look high-
...y, and walk contemptibly, it will asto-
...ish you to see Gods Judgments a pou-
...ing out upon you, and his wrath wax
...ot against you, till there be no remedy.
O do but see that Text, *Jer.* 51. 37.
And Babylon shall become heaps, a dwel-
...ing place for Dragons, an astonishment
...nd an hissing, without an Inhabitant:
Thus it will be with the ungodly at that
...day.   E 4   2. It

2. It will be a day of terror to tho[se] that know not God, and that obey n[ot] the Gospel of Christ; the terrors [of] God will be upon such, as it was upo[n] those Cities, *Gen.* 35. 5. O ye gracele[ss] persons, that now fear not God, n[or] tremble at his word, he will make yo[u] then tremble as he did *Belshazer*, whe[n] he beheld the hand-writing, Dan. 5. [6] *Then the Kings Countenance was change[d] and his thoughts troubled him, so that t[he] joints of his loins were loosed, and h[is] knees smote one against another.* O y[e] Drunkards and Swearers, you that de[-] spise reproofs, and hate instruction, an[d] set at nought all Gods counsel, kno[w] this, that the *day of Gods Wrath* will b[e] a day of terror to you, which will mak[e] your hearts to sink within you, you[r] countenance to change, your joints to b[e] loosed, and your ears to tingle, when th[e] terrors of the Almighty set themselve[s] in array against you. Therefore saith th[e] Apostle, 2 *Cor.* 5. 11. *Knowing therefor[e] the terrors of the Lord, we perswade men[.]*

3dly, This *day of Gods Wrath*, wil[l]
b[e]

The great Day of his Wrath.

a day of Distress to the wicked, when your fear shall come as desolation, and your destruction as a whirlwind, when distress and anguish cometh upon you, *Prov.* 1. 27. so see that in *Zeph.* 1. 15. That day is a day of wrath, a day of trouble and distress, a day of wastness and desolation, a day of darkness and gloominess, a day of clouds and thick darkness: *And I will bring distress upon men, that they shall walk like blind men, because they have sinned against the Lord, and their blood shall be poured out as dust, and their flesh as the dung, neither their Silver nor their Gold shall be able to deliver them in the day of the Lords wrath.* O the distress that ungodly persons will be in at this day, which will make them cry to the Rocks and Mountains to fall on them, and hide them from the face of him that sitteth on the Throne, and from the wrath of the Lamb. The God of Heaven will bring distress upon all sorts of men, which shall be found ungodly, and their honor shall not deliver them, nor their Gold

Gold deliver them, nor their Silver deliver them, nor the greatness of their multitudes deliver them, but distress will come upon them as it did upon Saul, 1 Sam. 28. 15. *And Saul answered, I am in sore distress, the Philistines make War against me, and God is departed from me, and answereth me neither by Prophesies, nor by dreams.* See Luk. 21. 23. *And there shall be great distress in the Land, and wrath upon this people.* Can you hear this, and not tremble at it, O you that are prophane?

Fourthly, This day of Gods wrath will be a day of great contempt to the ungodly, the Lord of Hosts hath purposed it, to stain the pride of glory, and to bring into contempt all the honorable of the Earth, Isa. 23. 9. O! the Enemies of the Lord, and such as oppose his Truth, will be then hissed at. O do but see that place Jer. 51. 37. *And Babylon shall become heaps, a dwelling place for Dragons, an astonishment and an hissing, without an Inhabitant.* The Lord will pour contempt upon all sorts of men,

men, who have sided with the Whore of *Babylon*, and drunk of her Cup, they will not know whither to go, nor where to hide their heads; but every one will hiss at them, and have them in derision, saying, These are they who said, It is in vain to serve the Lord, and what profit is there in the keeping of his Ordinances, and in walking mournfully before the Lord of Hosts? who counted Saints Sots, and godliness to be madness, therefore will they be contemptible before the Lord, Angels and good men. O think of this, you that speak proudly, and talk contemptuously against God and his People, know assuredly, That God will speak to you in his wrath, and vex you in his sore displeasure: *He that sitteth in the Heavens shall laugh, the Lord shall have you in derision*, Psal. 2.3,4.

Fifthly, This *day of Gods wrath* will be a day of great destruction; *Have ye not asked them that go by the way? and do ye not know their tokens, That the wicked is reserved to the day of destruction, they shall be brought forth to the day of wrath,*
Job

Job 21. 29, 30. In this day the Lord will destroy both evil persons, and evil things; men, and their Idols; men, and their Inventions, *Every plant which is not of Gods planting, shall be pluckt up, & the Lord alone shall be exalted in that day, and the Idols he shall utterly abolish; in that day a man shall cast his Idols of Silver, and his Idols of Gold which they have made each one for himself to worship, to the Moles and to the Bats, to go into the Clefts of the Rocks, and into the tops of the ragged Rocks, for fear of the Lord, and for the glory of his Majesty, when he ariseth to shake terribly the Earth*, Isa. 2. 18, 20, 21. All false ways, false worships, and false doctrines, shall fall in that day; this day will be a reaping day, God will empty the earth, as the Prophet Isaiah speaks, c. 24. 1, 2, 3. *Behold, the Lord maketh the earth empty, & maketh it wast, and turneth it upside-down, and scattereth abroad the Inhabitants thereof, and it shall be as with the people, so with the Priest; as with the servant, so with the Master; as with the Maid, so with her Mistress; as with*

with the Buyer, so with the Seller; as with the Lender, so with the Borrower; as with the taker of Usury, so with the giver of Usury to him; *the land shall be utterly emptied, and utterly spoiled; for the Lord hath spoken this Word.* See Joel 3.13,14. *Put ye in the sickle, for the Harvest is ripe; come, get you down, for the Press is full, the fats overflow, for the wickedness is great, Multitudes, multitudes in the valley of Derision; for the day of the Lord is near in the Valley of Derision.* So in Rev. 14.15. the Angels are appointed to reap down the Earth. O let every one that hears (or reads) these sayings, let them hear, and fear, and tremble at them, for this will be a day of great destruction to the wicked and ungodly.

Sixthly and lastly, This will be a day of great Wrath, as it is said in the words of my Text, *For the great day of his Wrath is come:* but who may abide the day of his coming and who shall stand when he appeareth? For he is like a refiners fire. O beloved! this is not the day of mans wrath, men have had their day

day of reigning, and raging, and lording it over Gods people, but that's over and gone, and now Gods day is come, and this is the day of his wrath, and wo to the Earth, and wo to the Sea, and wo to the whore of *Babylon*; for the hour of her Judgment is come. O Beloved, Gods wrath will be very terrible to the wicked.

1. It will tear them in pieces like a Lion, *For I will be unto Ephraim as a lion, and as a young lion to the house of Judah: I, even I, will tear and go away, I will take away and none shall rescue him.* Hosea 5. 14. so *Job.* 16. 9. *The Lord teareth me in his wrath,* so Psal. 50. 22. *Now consider this, ye that forget God, lest I tear you in pieces, and there be none to deliver.*

2. It consumes like fire: for behold the day cometh that shall burn like an oven, and all the proud, yea, and all that do wickedly, shall be stubble, and the day that cometh, shall burn them up, saith the Lord of Hosts, that it shall leave them neither root nor branch, *Mal.* 4. 1.

The great Day of his Wrath. 63

[1]. *Therefore have I poured out mine in-[dig]nation upon them, I have consumed them [with] the fire of my wrath,* Ezek. 22. 31.

[2]. It swallows up like a Dragon, he [ha]th devoured me, he hath crushed me, [he] hath swallowed me up like a Dragon, [Jer.]51.34. *Thou shalt make them as a fie[ry] Oven in the time of thine anger, the [Lor]d shall swallow them up in his wrath, [and] the fire shall devour them,* Psal. 21. 9. [And] the wrath of the Almighty is that [wh]ich tears like a Lyon, consumes like [fire], and swallows up like a Dragon; and [the]refore it is called (in the Scripture) [fier]ce wrath, 2 *Kings* 23. 26. See *Psal.* [78.]49. He cast upon them the fierce[nes]s of his anger, wrath and indignati[on], and trouble. So in *Rev.* 16. 19. it [is] said, *And the great City was divided in[to] three parts, and the Cities of the Na[tion]s fell, and great Babylon came in re[me]mbrance before God, to give unto her [the] Cup of the Wine of the fierceness of [his] wrath.* Thus beloved, I have shew[ed] you the nature and property of this [gr]eat day spoken of in my Text:

1. A

The great Day of his Wrath.

1. A day of Astonishment.
2. A day of Terror.
3. A day of Distress.
4. A day of Contempt.
5. A day of Destruction.
6. A day of Wrath.

I shall now come in the third place, shew you who they are that will not able to stand in this great Day.

First, Such as are prophane, will n be able to stand in this great Day, b say to the Mountains, Fall on us; and the Hills, Cover us, Luke 23.30. *cause they have filled the midst of t with violence, and thou hast sinned, ther fore I will cast thee as prophane out of t Mountain of God, and I will destroy th O covering Cherub, from the midst of t stones of Fire,* Ezek. 28.16. so Rom. 2. *Tribulation and anguish upon every soul man that doth evil.* O ye prophane, that now wallow in your sins, as the s in the mire, and eat up sin, as they bread, and drink up iniquity like wate

[...]! let me tell you, you will not be [ab]le to stand in the day of wrath, nor [in] the day of Judgement, but destructi[on] will be your end, and everlasting mi[ser]y your portion. O that such would [bu]t consider these two places of Scrip[tu]re, Phil. 3. 19. *Whose end is destruction, whose God is their belly, whose glory is in their shame, who mind earthly things.* So [al]so that in 1 Cor. 6. 9, 10. *Know ye not, [th]at the unrighteous shall not inherit the [K]ingdom of God: Be not deceived,*

Neither Fornicators,
Nor Idolaters,
Nor Adulterers,
Nor Effeminate,
Nor abusers of themselves with mankind,
Nor Thieves,
Nor Covetous,
Nor Drunkards,
Nor Revilers,
Nor Extortioners, shall inherit the Kingdom of God.

F   Though

Though these men may now carry [it] out with a high hand, as if they ha[d] made a Covenant with Death, and wit[h] Hell they were at an agreement; Bu[t] your Covenant with Death shall be di[s]annulled, and your Agreement with He[ll] shall not stand, when the overflowin[g] scourge shall pass thorow, then ye sha[ll] be trodden down by it, *Isa.* 28.15, 18.

Secondly, Such as are ignorant, wi[ll] not be able to stand in this great day o[f] Gods Wrath, when the Lord Jesus sha[ll] be revealed from Heaven with his migh[ty] Angels, in flaming fire, taking vengeance on them that know not God, and that obey not the Gospel of ou[r] Lord Jesus Christ, who shall be punish[ed] with everlasting destruction from th[e] presence of the Lord, and from th[e] glory of his Power, 2 *Thes.* 1.7, 8, 9. O you that are ignorant and blind, d[o] you hear this? you are some of thos[e] who will not be able to stand in thi[s] great day, but say to the Rocks, Fall o[n] us, and hide us from the face of him tha[t] sittet[h]

[...]eth on the Throne, and from the [wr]ath of the Lamb. Beloved, I told [yo]u in the morning, That Ignorance is [o]ne of those cursed sins that bars and [b]olts Christ out of the heart, it is that [w]hich shuts them out from having mer[c]y and favour with the Lord: See Isa.27 [1]1. *For it is a people of no understand[in]g, therefore he that made them, will [ha]ve no mercy on them; and he that form[ed] them, will shew them no favour.*

Thirdly, Such as have sided with An[ti]christ against Christ, will not be able [to] stand in this great day; such as have [d]runk of the Whores Cup of Fornica[t]ion, shall drink of the Cup of Gods [In]dignation, which is poured out with[o]ut mixture: *If any man worship the [B]east and his Image, & receive his mark in [hi]s forehead, or in his hand, the same shall [d]rink of the Wine of the wrath of God, [w]hich is poured out without mixture, into [th]e Cup of his indignation, and he shall be [t]ormented with fire and brimstone, in the [p]resence of the holy Angels, and in the presence of the Lamb,* Rev. 14. 9, 10. Beloved! all those who have been partakers with her in sinning, shall be partakers with her in suffering; therefore come out of her my people, that ye be not partakers of her sins, and that ye receive not of her plagues, *Rev.* 18. 4. All that cursed brood of *Rome*, with all the Antichristian crew, will not be able to stand in this great day of Gods wrath, but will be consumed like fuel, and devoured as stubble fully dry; see *Nahum* 1. 9, 10. *What do ye imagine against the Lord? he will make an utter end, affliction shall not rise up the second time; for while they be folden together as thorns, and while they are drunken as drunkards, they shall be devoured as stubble fully dry;* so that all those who have assisted Antichrist against Christ,

 Against his Government,
 Against his Gospel,
 Against his Spirit,
 Against his Worship,
 Against his Ministers,
 Against his Members,

And

And against his Glorious Cause;

I say, they will not be able to stand in this day of Gods wrath: but cry to the Rocks and the Mountains to fall on them, and to hide them from the face of him that sitteth on the Throne, and from the wrath of the Lamb, *Rev.* 19. 19, 20, 21.

4. Such as have a form of Godliness, and deny the power thereof, will not be able to stand in this *Great Day of Gods Wrath*; Having a form of Godliness but denying the power thereof, from such turn away, 2 *Tim.* 3. 5. All idle and slothful professors, who have nothing of God, nor nothing of Christ, nor nothing of the Spirit, nor nothing of the power of the word in them, having only a notion or formal profession; such I say, will not be able to stand in this Day. See *Rom.* 2. 17. Behold, thou art called a *Jew*, and restest in the Law, and makest thy boast of God, and art confident that thou thy self art a guider of the blind, an instructer of the foolish, a teacher of babes, which hast the form of know-

F 3   ledg,

ledg and of the truth, in the law, b[ut]
mark what God saith to such, ver. 2[3.]
*Thou that makest thy boast of t[he]
Law, through breaking of the L[aw]
dishonourest thou God? For the na[me]
of God is blasphemed among the Ge[n-]
tiles through you.* O! are there n[ot]
many amongst us, who profess G[od]
in words, but deny him in works? w[ho]
have a name to live, and are dea[d,]
who have a form, but not the pow[er,]
who have all without, and nothing wit[h-]
in? like to those in *Mat.* 7. there spok[en]
of by Christ, ver 22. *Many will say to [me]
in that day Lord, Lord, have we not prop[he-]
sied in thy Name, and in thy Name ha[ve]
cast out Devils, and in thy Name done [ma-]
ny wonderful works?* Ver. 23. *And t[hen]
will I profess unto them, I never kn[ew]
you, Depart from me ye that work i[ni-]
quity.*

   5. Such as are Idle Shepherds, a[nd]
blind Guides, will not be able to stan[d in]
this great day of Gods wrath, but wil[l cry]
to the rocks and the mountains to fal[l on]
them, and to hide them from the f[ace]

of him that sitteth on the Throne, and from the Wrath of the Lamb. For this, see a few Scriptures amongst many, what the Lord our God speaketh against idle Shepherds, and blind Guides, Who feed themselves, and not the Flock of Christ. See *Ezek.* 34. 2, 3, 4. *Thus saith the Lord God unto the Shepherds, Wo be to the shepherds of Israel, that do feed themselves: should not the Shepherds feed the flock? Ye eat the Fat, and ye clothe you with the Wool; Ye kill them that are fed, but ye feed not the flock; The diseased have ye not strengthned, neither have ye healed that which was sick, neither have ye bound up that which was broken, neither have ye brought again that which was driven away; neither have ye sought that which was lost; but with force and with cruelty have ye ruled them. Therefore, O ye Shepherds, hear the word of the Lord, Thus saith the Lord God, Behold, I am against the Shepherds, and I well require my flock at their hand, and cause them to cease from feeding the flock, neither shall the Shepherds feed themselves*

any more. *For I will deliver my Flo[ck]
from their mouth, that they may not [be]
meat for them*, ver. 9. 10. *For bot[h]
Prophet and Priest are prophane, yea, in m[y]
house have I found their wickedness, sait[h]
the Lord. Therefore thus saith the Lor[d]
of Hosts, concerning the Prophets, behol[d]
I will feed them with wormwood, and ma[ke]
them drink the water of Gall: for fro[m]
the Prophets of Jerusalem, is prophanene[ss]
gone forth into all the land*, Jer. 23. 1[4,]
15, 16. See also Hos. 4. from ver. 1, t[o]
11. Mark also what our Lord Jesu[s]
Christ saith, *Mat.* 23. of idle Shep[-]
herds and blind Guides, vers. 14. W[oe]
*unto you Scribes and Pharisees, Hypocrites[,]
For ye devour Widows houses, and for [a]
pretence make long prayers, therefore y[e]
shall receive the greater damnation.* Thu[s]
you see, beloved, that the Scripture[s]
with open mouth do speak forth the de[-]
solation, and calamities which will befal[l]
idle Shepherds, and blind Guides in tha[t]
day; and if they cannot stand when hi[s]
wrath is kindled but a little, O wha[t]
will they do when his wrath shall com[e]
upon

upon them to the utmost, even the fierceness of his wrath? then will they not be able to stand.

6thly. Such as are *Hypocrites* will not be able to stand in this day of Gods wrath, but desire if it were possible to hide themselves in the Dens and Caves of the earth. And the people shall be as the burning of lime, as thorns cut up shall they be burnt in the fire. Hear ye that are afar off what I have done, and ye that are near, acknowledge my Might; The sinners in *Zion* are afraid, fearfulness hath surprised the Hypocrites: Who among us shall dwell with devouring fire? Who among us shall dwell with everlasting burnings? See *Job* 8. 13. *So are the paths of all that forget God, and the Hypocrites hope shall perish.* ver. 14. *Whose hope shall be cut off, and whose trust shall be a Spiders web.* ver. 15. *He shall lean upon his house but it shall not stand, he shall hold it fast, but it shall not endure.* O thou hypocrite, who ever thou art, notwithstanding thou hast got the talking part of Religion, and

makest

makest a shew of Godliness, yet all the while thou art a dissembler in thy heart. See *Jer.* 42. 20. 21. 22. *For ye dissembled in your hearts, when ye sent me unto the Lord your God, saying, Pray for us unto the Lord our God, and according unto all that the Lord our God shall say, declare unto us, and we will do it. And now I have this day declared it to you, but ye have not obeyed the Voice of the Lord your God, nor any thing for the which he hath sent me unto you. Now therefore know certainly, that ye shall dye by the Sword, by the Famine, and by the Pestelence, in the place whither ye desire to go, and to sojourn.* Do you hear this, ye that are hypocrites, that God hates such, and will punish them with great punishments? He will cut them asunder, and give them their portion with Reprobates and Cast-awayes, in everlasting burnings, *Matth.* 24. 51.

    7. And lastly, All such as love not the Lord Jesus Christ in truth and sincerity, will not be able to stand in this day of Gods Wrath; Whether they be Turks or

or Jews, Papists or Protestants, bond, or free, all is one, for they will not be able to stand if they love not the Lord Jesus Christ; See 1 *Cor.* 16.22. *If any man love not the Lord Jesus Christ, let him be Anathema, Maranatha.* O beloved! all those who shall be found unbelievers, unconverted, and unregenerate in this Day of Gods Wrath, be they Kings, or great men, rich men or chief Captains, or mighty men, or be they bondmen, or free-men, they shall all cry to the Mountains and Rocks, saying, *Fall on us, and hide us from the face of him that sitteth on the Throne, and from the wrath of the Lamb; for the great day of his Wrath is come.*

Thus beloved, I have shewed you briefly in seven particulars; who they are that will not be able to stand in *the day of Gods wrath.*

1. The Prophane.
2. The Ignorant.
3. They that side with Antichrist against Christ.

4. The formal professor.

5. The Idle Shepherds and bli[nd] Guides.

6. The Hypocrites.

7. And lastly, They that love not t[he] Lord Jesus.

Obj. But beloved, it may be you will s[ay,] If none of these will be able to stand, w[ho] then will?

Answ. I Answer; All those who sha[ll] be found having on their wedding ga[r]ments, and in the Spirit of the Lam[b] will be able to stand in this day, and the[y] are these.

1. *They that overcome,* Rev. 2. 1[1.] Chap. 3. 21. Chap. 12. 11. Chap. 21. 7[.]

2. *They that keep the Commandment[s] of God, and have the Testimony of Jesu[s] Christ,* Rev. 12. 17. Chap. 6. 9.

3. *They that stand with the Lamb,* Rev. 14. 1. chap. 17. 14.

4. *They that have their Fathers nam[e] written in their forehead,* Rev. 14. 1[.]

5. *They that sing a new song.* Revel. 14. 2.

6. *They that are redeemed from the* earth, ver. 3.

7. *They*

The great Day of his Wrath. 77

7. *They that follow the Lamb whither-*
[so]ever he goeth, ver. 4.

8. *They that are not defiled with the*
[pol]lutions of the Whore of Babylon, and in
[the]ir mouths is found no guile, ver. 5.

[N]ow beloved, these are they who will
[be] able to stand in that great day of
[G]ods Wrath, when others will not
[be] able, but call to the rocks and moun-
[ta]ins to fall on them.

[I] shall now proceed in the fourth place,
[to] the *Use* and *Application* of this point.

Use. 1. And first of all by way of In-
[for]mation; If it be so, that the greatest
[par]t of Men and Women will not be a-
[bl]e to stand in This day of Gods Wrath,
[th]en this may inform us of three things:

1. That as men have had their day,
[so] God will have his day: men have had
[the]ir day of sinning, God will have his
[da]y of punishing: men have had their day
[of] treasuring up of wrath, God will have
[hi]s day of pouring out of Wrath: men
[ha]ve had their Day of defiling, God
[wi]ll have his day of refining: men have
[ha]d their day of fornication, God will
have

78   *The great Day of his Wrath.*

have his day of Indignation: *For the day of the Lord is near upon all the Heathen, as thou hast done, it shall be done unto thee; thy reward shall return upon thine own head*, Oba. 15.

2. That though God beareth with sinners in the day of his patience, yet he will not bear with them in the day of his wrath. *Go through the City, and smite, let not your eye spare, neither have ye pity,* Ezek. 9. 5. O beloved! in the day of Gods patience, he beareth with you, and waiteth to be gracious: O how many hundred years hath *God* bore with the whore of *Babylon*, notwithstanding her great provocations and wickedness; but now in the day of his Wrath, the Lord will not spare her, nor shew pity to her, but pour out his Wrath and Indignation upon her to the utmost; Therefore shall her Plagues come in one day, death and mourning, and famine, and she shall be utterly burnt with fire: For strong is the Lord God who judgeth her. *Rev.* 18. 8. O see that terrible word *Isa.* 42. 13, 14. *The Lord shall go forth as a mighty*

man,

The great Day of his Wrath. 79

man, he shall stir up Jealousie like a man of War, he shall cry, yea, roar; he shall prevail against his Enemies. *I have long time holden my peace; I have been still and refrained my self: Now will I cry like a travelling woman; I will destroy and devour at once:* Do you see this sinners, how God is resolved to proceed against you in the day of his Wrath, though he bear with you in the day of his Patience?

3dly, This day of Gods wrath will be a very dreadful and terrible day to the wicked, as appears by what hath been said. O sinners! it will be a day of Astonishment, a Day of Terror, a day of Distress, a day of Contempt, a day of Destruction, and a day of Wrath: O! it will be a day of Darkness and gloominess, a day of Clouds and thick darkness, Joel 2.2. *The great day of the Lord is near, it is near, and hasteth greatly, even the voice of the day of the Lord; the mighty man shall cry there bitterly; that day is a day of wrath, a day of trouble and distress, a day of wastness and desolation,*
a day

a day of darkness and gloominess, a day of Clouds and thick darkness, Zeph. 1.14,15. O who is able to express the terror of the Almighty in this day of his Wrath! O that every soul that hears me this day, would lay to heart, and consider with themselves, that they may be able to stand in this day of Gods wrath. And so much for this *Use* of *Information*.

Use 2. By way of *Examination* and *Self-tryal*.

O Friends! how much doth it concern you and me, to examine our standing, that we may be able to stand in the day of Gods wrath, which is coming so fast upon us. O! you see how that his wrath is but a little kindled, and yet how hard a matter is it for men to stand, and to abide it! Thousands have been sent to their Graves by it, and many hundreds have left their habitations, because of it, and are fled out of the City, into several parts of this Kingdom for refuge. O what a sad and doleful

place

hath this City been for several [days] past! The greatest Trade which [hath] been here amongst us, was to bury [the] dead, and tend the sick. O now my [br]ethren, if this little be so much, what [wi]ll it be when the great day of his wrath is come! who will then be able to [sta]nd? O therefore, examine your selves, [an]d try your selves, examine your faith, [w]hether it be true; your knowledg, whe[t]her it be sanctified; your hope, whether [it] be purified; your love, whether it be [si]ncere; your evidences, whether they be [so]und; your hearts, whether they be [gra]cious; your desires, whether they be [ho]ly; your ends, whether they be right, [an]d your conversations, whether they [be] heavenly, that you may be able to [sta]nd in the day of Wrath, in the day of [D]eath, and in the day of Judgement, *Cor.* 13.5.

Use 3. Thirdly, By way of *Exhorta-*[ti]on.

And I shall be brief, lest I should in[tru]de too much upon your patience; but [I] hope you will not think the time long,

G for

for it may be the last Sermon that I ma[y]
preach, or your hear. Well (Beloved[)]
Is it so, That the greatest part of me[n]
and women will not be able to stand [in]
the day of God's Wrath, give me leav[e]
therefore to exhort you to these thre[e]
things:

First, You that are sinners, to repen[t]
of your sins; *for he that confesseth an[d]
forsaketh, shall have mercy*, Prov. 28.1[3]
*He that covereth his sins, shall not prosper[,]
but he that confesseth and forsaketh them[,]
shall have mercy. Happy is the man tha[t]
feareth alway; but he that hardneth hi[s]
heart, shall fall into mischief.* O sinners[,]
you have grievously sinned against God[,]
you have deserved as many Hells, as yo[u]
have commtited sins; you have sinne[d]
against his mercies, you have abused hi[s]
patience, you have resisted his Spirit[,]
you have disobeyed his Gospel, you hav[e]
made light of his Ministers, and yo[u]
have hated his Members. O sinners! al[l]
this have you done, and yet the Lord
hath spared you; and though you have
sinned at so high a rate, yet God doth
give

give you space to repent: O let his goodness lead you to repentance, that you dye not in your sins. O therefore for God's sake, and Christ's sake, be prevailed withal; why will ye dye, seeing God would have you live? Why will ye damn your selves? Why will ye go to Hell, seeing God would have you go to Heaven? O do but see what the Lord saith, Isa. 1. 18. *Come sinner*, saith the Lord, *and let thee and I reason together, though thy sins be as scarlet, they shall be as snow: though they be red as crimson, they shall be white like wool.* Verily, if you have not hearts of stone, methinks these words should melt you, to see the love, the pity, the mercy and willingness of God to do your souls good.

Secondly, Let me exhort you, to get an Interest in the Lord Jesus, that you may be able to stand in the day of his Wrath: O sinners! there will be no standing before Christ, without an Interest in Christ. O sinners! go to Christ, his Promises are open to you, his Arms are open to embrace you, his Spirit is

ready to assist you, and his people
ready to own you, and his Angels
ready to attend you, and Heaven it[self]
is ready to receive you. O sinners! [if]
you will but come to Christ, you sh[all]
be reconciled to the Father, justified [by]
the Son, you shall be sanctified by t[he]
Spirit, you shall be delivered from wra[th,]
you shall be made the Children of Go[d,]
you shall have your names enrolled [in]
the Book of Life; and finally, you sh[all]
be received into everlasting glory at t[he]
end of your days. O therefore let t[his]
prevail with you to go to Christ f[or]
Light, for Life, for Grace, for Strengt[h,]
and for Comfort and Peace, that of [his]
fulness you may receive grace for grac[e,]
Iohn 1. 16.

   Thirdly, And lastly, Let me now e[x]hort you (who are dead to sin, separat[ed]
from the World, espoused to Christ, r[e]conciled to the Father) to walk worth[y]
of God, who hath called you to h[is]
Kingdom and Glory, 1 *Thess.* 2. 12. [O]
ye precious Saints, let me exhort you [to]
keep your Lamps burning, your Loi[ns]
                          girde[d]

[...]ded, your Lives holy, and your [hea]rts upright, your Judgements [sou]nd, your Consciences pure, and [yo]ur Garments unspotted; and be not [trou]bled at Gods dealings, and Dispen-[sat]ions, though he take away from you [tho]se that are precious to you; for as he [sen]ds the Wicked to Hell, that they [ma]y dishonor him no more; so he takes [awa]y the Righteous to Heaven, that [the]y may glorifie him more there, seems [to]be four Reasons why God sweeps a-[wa]y the Righteous with the wicked by [th]e Pestilence.

1. Because they have finished their [w]ork.
2. From the evil to come.
3. For the humbling of the rest [wh]ich remain behind.
4. For the hardning of the Wicked.

Therefore ye precious Saints, you [ou]ght to be quiet, and to submit to the [w]ill of God, and to say with *David*, *[I w]as dumb and opened not my mouth, be-*
G 3 *cause*

cause thou didst it, Psal. 39. 9. Now I beseech you, both Saints and sinners,
consider of those things, and the G[od]
of Heaven give you understanding
all things which concerns his glory, a[nd]
your eternal good.

The End of the Second Sermon.

Watch AND PRAY.

MARK 14. 38.

Watch and Pray, lest ye enter into temptation.

AS Christ is the Churches Friend, so Satan is the Churches Enemy,
    Her greatest Enemy,
Her cruellest Enemy,
Her worst Enemy,
Her continual Enemy.

He that makes War against the Remnant of her Seed which keeps the Commands of God, and have the Testimony of Jesus, *Rev.* 12.17.

The Devil envieth our happiness, and seeks our ruine,

1. By tempting of us, 1 *Cor.* 7.5.
2. By persecuting of us, *Rev.* 2.10.
3. By accusing of us, *Rev.* 12.10.
4. By hindering of us, 1 *Thess.* 2.18.
5. By beguiling of us, 2 *Cor.* 11.3.

O Beloved! the Devil is
The great Troubler of Saints,
The great Deceiver of Nations.
The great Devourer of Souls.
The great Enemy of all Mankind, who goeth about like a roaring Lyon, seeking whom he may devour, 1 *Peter* 5.9.

But now here is the Churches happiness, That Christ is her Friend, *Canticles* 5.16.

Her

Her greatest Friend,
Her dearest Friend,
Her loving Friend,
Her best Friend,
Her constant Friend,
Her sympathizing Friend,
Her mighty Friend, by his Blood she overcomes the Devil.

By his Graces she resists the Devil.

By his Might she treads him under her feet:

And by Faith in his Word she quenches all the fiery darts of the Devil.

O! though Satan hates us, Christ loves us; though Satan condemns us, Christ justifies us.

Though Satan accuses us, Christ clears us.

Though Satan tempts us, Christ strengthens us.

Though Satan seeks to destroy us, Christ preserves us.

Though Satan buffets us, Christ assists us;

1. By

1. By his Spirit.
2. By his Promises.
3. By his Graces.
4. By his Presence.
5. By his Word.
6. By his Intercession.
7. By his Power.
8. By his Ministers.
9. By his Examples.
10. By his Prayers.

O! The Lord Jesus hath a great love to us, and care of us, and therefore he counsels us in the words of the Text, *To watch and pray, lest we enter into temtation.*

These are the words of our Lord Jesus to his Disciples, they having been slumbering and sleeping, when Christ had commanded them to *Watch.*

They contain, first, A supposition of their entering into temptation, upon which Christ grounds a Mandatory Exhortation, shewing them the way how to avoid it, in these words, *Watch and Pray*, &c.

Hence

Hence we may raise these two points of Doctrine:

Doct. 1. That a Child of God is attended with temptations.

Doct. 2. That the only way to avoid the evil of temptation, is to watch and pray.

For the first of these we may observe this Method:
First, Of the Tempter.
Secondly, Of the Temptation.
Thirdly, Of the manner of their working, with the Reasons why they have so much power.

First, We have four several Tempters in Scripture.

1. God tempting man, *i.e.* trying and proving man, as in *Deut.* 8. 2. Thus God tempted *Abraham*, *Gen.* 22. 1. which is interpreted *Heb.* 11. 17. *By faith Abraham when he was tryed, offered up Isaac*, &c. This tempting is not to evil,

nor

nor for our hurt; but God tempteth upon these accounts:

1. For the Tryal of his peoples fear; as in that of *Abraham*, *Gen*. 22. 12. *For now I know that thou fearest God, seeing thou hast not with-held thine onely Son from me.*

2. God temps for the Tryal of their faith, he proves them in something that's near and dear to them; perhaps deprives them of some special necessary mercy, to see whether they can trust him, and believe in the want of it; whether they can live by faith upon the God of the mercies; when the mercies are gone; *As it is written; the Just shall live by faith*, *Hab*. 2. 4. *Rom*. 1. 17 and it is said of *Abraham*, when he was tryed, *he offered up Isaac*, *Heb*. 11. 17.

3. Again thirdly, the Lord tempts for the proof of their obedience, and thus the Lord speaks to *Abraham* after that tryal; *And in thy seed shall all the nations of the earth be blessed*; why? *because thou hast obeyed my voice*. In all this, the Lord seeth what is in our hearts, as he said to *Israel*, of old, *Deut*. 8. 2.

2. We

2. We may find man tempting God too, that is, provoking God to jealousie and wrath: Thus did the children of *Israel* at the waters of *Meribah*, *Deut. 6. 16. Ye shall not tempt the Lord your God. Exod. 17. 2. Wherefore do ye tempt the Lord?* but first of all, We tempt God when we doubt of his Power, as when we are in any strait or difficulty, we mistrust the power of God to deliver us, or bestow any mercy upon us which we stand in need of; as that Lord did on whose hand the King leaned, who said, *If the Lord would make windows in heaven, might this thing be? when God had promised, in time of famine, that on the morrow there should be plenty,* 2 Kings 7. 2.

Secondly, We tempt God, when we doubt of his Mercy; for God is mercy in the abstract; and it is a part of his glorious stile; therefore he cannot endure to lose so great a part of his honor, but is provoked by it.

Thirdly, When we call his faithfulness into question; what greater disparagement or more distastful to man, than to be wrongfully accused for falsifying his word? then how much greater provocation is it to the great God, to be impeached for breach of promise, and counted unfaithful, who cannot lye? *Heb.* 6.18.

4. Lastly, When we murmure at the hand of God, at any of his Judgments, thus *Israel* did at *Meribah*, *Exod.* 17.2,3 and this doth exceedingly inflame and excite the wrath of God: We cannot dispose for our selves, and yet we are angry at the providence of an All-wise God: We sin, and are troubled that God corrects us for sin.

3. In the next place, our Lusts are Tempters, as *Jam.* 1. 14. Every man is tempted, when he is drawn away of his own hearts lusts, and entised.. Our lusts strive within us to be sinfully satisfyed, and the flesh wars against the Spirit, the heart sometimes alluring; and this comes to pass,

1. By presenting some sinful object; It is good not to nourish such conceptions, but strangle them in their first appearance,

pearance, else sinful thoughts grow upon us.

2. By presenting some desirableness in the object: but be quick-sighted; sin, however it seems fair under some colourable pretence, is indeed, upon good deliberations, not at all to be desired; but sometimes it comes clothed in such a glorious Garb, as if it meant no harm, that you must be fain to flye to God by prayer against this temptation.

3. There's a perswasion to consent to the sin; but be not easily perswaded to offend your Father: Oh! how will our lusts gain upon us, if we do not resist! Strive with all your might; the greater your allurement to sin is, the greater the sin is; I appeal to Saints experience.

4. In the fourth and last place, we have the devil tempting man; he is called the Tempter, *Matt.* 4.1,3. *Mark* 1.13. And indeed this is the grand Tempter, that makes use of our lusts, as a subservient Organ or Instrument for his temptations against the soul; and indeed, were

it

it not for our Lusts, it would be in vain for Satan to tempt: As we see in Christ there was nothing within for Satan to take hold of, Christ being without sinful lusts, but Satan must come by word of mouth to tempt him, as *Matt.* 4.1,3. but here it might be enquired, How shall I know when Satan raiseth the temptation?

1. I answer; first, When it comes strongly and forcibly upon the soul, as it were, with a double power, even overthrowing the soul (almost) at the first encounter.

There's double strength in the stroke.

2. Secondly, When it is of long continuance, as that was which *Paul* besought the Lord thrice for, 2 *Cor.* 12.8. Satan stirs up the heart afresh, and the lusts of the heart: When the fire is ready to dye and go out, he blows it up again, adds life and strength to the temptation, which else could not last long. The Lusts they are the combustible matter, and Satan he inflames, and sets them on fire.

3. Third-

3. Thirdly, The Temptation, when though it may be weak at first, yet at length, by degrees, it grows stronger and stronger. Satan begins to reason with, and perswade the soul by plausible arguments.

4. Fourthly, We may perceive the working of that Serpent, the Devil; when the temptation is full of wiles and subtile delusions; *Ephes.* 16.11. 2 *Tim.* 3.16. *Rev.* 2.24. The more intricate and full of subtilty the temptation is, the more cause there is to suspect, Satan is very busie for the insnaring of the soul.

5. Lastly, The more it is in direct opposition to God in his commands, or the like; we may be the more sure it is of Satans framing: For the heart and its lusts seek for satisfaction, and then are still, (if Satan join not) though God be not so directly opposed: But the Devil strikes always at God in his temptations; or if not always, yet most freequently.

H   Thus

Thus much for the Tempter; now for the temptation it self. There are several sorts of temptations; but to reduce them all to these three heads; they do concern, and strike at

First of all, God, this being Satans great aim, to oppse God; as two mortal enemies, always in direct opposition one to the other; and thus he tempts either,

1. As to the Being of God, calling in question the very truth of the Essence of the great God, causing the soul to doubt whether there be a God or no, like *Pharoah*, *Who is the Lord, &c. Exod.* 5. 2.

But secondly, Some temptations touch upon the nature of God, as to the manner of his being, the mystery of three distinct persons, as to their offices and operations, in one individual God-head, God the Father, God the Son, God the holy Spirit; and yet all but one God blessed for ever. Again, as to those divine, inseparable attributes of God, his in-

independecy, purity, immutability, greatness, & eternity; his goodness grace, mercy, love, patience, and justice. I say, somtimes a doubting of these things, is our temptation; yea, and could Satan prevail, we should flatly deny his Being, Nature, Properties, and all. Look sternly on, and resist strongly such temptations as these, which do immediately and presumptuously intrench upon Gods Soveraign and just Prerogative. And, if I mistake not, a great device of Satans in this Stratagem is, to perswade the creature from all dependency upon a Creator, that so being left to it self, and standing upon its own strength, he may more easily destroy it. For what's the creature without the Creators power.

Again, Some temptations touch our Spiritual Being. Such as are an evil heart of unbelief, mistrusting the Grace of God, despairing of the goodness of our condition; Satan would fain raize the very foundation of spiritual existence, Adoption, Justification. and hopes of Salvation; it is his great design to shake

shake the very ground-work of this building, and to perswade, that all's false. But this temptation is fruitless, when we build aright upon a right foundation, by faith accompanied with repentance from dead works, upon Christ Jesus, as the alone Author and Meritorious Cause of our Justification and eternal glorification.

3. Lastly, Satan by his fiery darts strikes at our well-being, to disturb our peace; by the omission of some duty, or commission of some sin; When he finds he cannot prevail to destroy our being, then he would deprive us of wel-being, our joy & comfort. But know, though these temptations may trouble us, yet shall they never destroy us.

The manner of temptation.

Now for the manner of these Temptations, how they work.

1. When we fall under any want, strait, change of providence, or the like; then is a time for temptation to work. As when Christ had fasted, and was an hungred, then comes the Tempter; If thou be the Son of God, command

mand that these stones be made bread, *Mat.* 4. 3.

2. When we are first turning from sin to God, then we are sure to meet with a Tempter, Satan will be busie.

3. When we are troubled, dejected, disconsolated, either to the outward or inward estate, then beware of Satan's temptations, he will be furthering our disquietments.

4. When we are arrived to some good hopes through grace, to some confidence in the mercy of God the Father through his Son Jesus Christ; then also shall we find the battering assaults of Satan to shake our confidence. But be sure always that the grounds of your confidence be good, established upon that everlasting Rock Jesus Christ. For if I mistake not in my observation, there are two great Rocks, which Satan strives to split a soul upon, Presumption, and Despair: Sometimes endeavouring to cause souls to flatter up themselves, and think Grace is theirs, Christ is theirs, and all is theirs, when it is
no-

nothing so, but by this he might carry them blind to Hell, hood-winking their souls so, that they never come to see thoroughly, that they are in a bad condition, but think always their condition good. The other Rock is Despair; Satan striving, if he cannot blind them as he doth the other presumptuous souls, yet to make them go sorrowing all their days, thinking they shall never obtain that mercy which others think they always had.

5. Satan suits his temptations to our dispositions; he hath various objects for divers spirits, for the proud, haughty soul, for the lustful heart; for the covetous worldling; for the Prodigal Son; for the rash giddy brain; for the sluggish drone; for the melancholly person; for the light chearful spirit; especially these two either sinking the one in the terrible waves of black and dreadfull thoughts, or tossing and lifting up the other with the wind of foolish phantasie. Oh! What black apprehensions shall the one have of it self and God; and what light and slight

slight thoughts, the other, of the present state, and of Eternity.

6. Lastly, Satan aims to lull the soul asleep in carnal security: and to this end presents great sins as small, and little sins (if any there be) as none at all: But sometimes he will add by Temptation, as it were a multiplying-glass to the soul, so that then every sin looks with a ghastly countenance, is thought to be the sin against the holy spirit, an unpardonable sin.

Having thus shewn how, and upon what occasions Satan works; I shall take occasion to inquire, why they have so much power, as many times to prevail?

1. Because of the Tempters Power, he is perhaps too strong for the soul.

2. Because of the Tempters Policy; If he cannot prevail by open force, the soul being well and strongly grounded; then he invades by subtile devices, and secret stratagems, so that the soul cannot escape by strength onely; and therefore

fore (wanting Wisdom to evade his cunningly framed Arguments) is bafled by him, and overthrown.

3. The enticing nature of the Tempters baits; as, to instance in one case: Oh how many poor sincere souls, yet guilty of too much curiosity, have been entangled by curiously glorious, and gloriously curious tenets, which were no better then the devillish Temptations of that Hellish Tempter! how many (which yet is strange to think, though there is reason to fear it) nay, after their seemingly comfortable, really comfortless wandering walkings in thought-wayes of Truth, have cause to sit down, and set down their steps, marking for every step, a sin; and for every sin, letting fall a tear of blood.

4. Temptations often prevail by reason of the strength of corruptions, which the Tempters work upon. Were there no corruptions, there would be few or no temptations; I am sure, they should not prevail.

5. Lastly,

5. Lastly, The Tempters prevalency, proceeds from the weakness and low estate of the inward man. Sin is never at a higher flood, then when Grace is at a low ebb; It is a hard matter (believe experience) to keep the soul from sinking at such a time. Nothing more easie then to thrust one under water, when the depth of the water is more than the height of the man.

Obj. But now to make sure the Doctrinal part, I shall lay down some reasons why the people of God are thus attended with temptations; for it is a natural Objection against this point, *Why will the Lord, who is so merciful of his people, suffer them to be thus used and buffeted by temptations?*

Ans. I answer, in general, on Gods behalf, that he is never the less tender in it, as will appear in particular, thus:

1. Because one end seems to be this, That they might know themselves the better, and see what they are naturally; were it not for temptation, we should not come to know our own corruption;
we

we see by this, what Lust is most prevalent in us, according to that in *Heb.*12.1. *The sin that doth so easily beset us*; and what Satan makes most use of against us; we learn by this our own weakness to resist, without assisting Grace.

2. Again, it is for a Saints exercise: This tempted condition is Gods Artillery, his School of Arms, wherein God brings up his Children, trains them, and instructs them how to clasp on their Helmet of Salvation, to put on the brestplate of Righteousness, to hold out the Shield of Faith, to brandish the Sword of the Spirit, in a word, how to put on the Lord Jesus Christ, even our whole Armour of Righteousness.

3. That we might know our Enemies, that we may be the more watchful over Satan, Sin and the World.

4. That we might long to be at home with our Father; that we might be weaned from the milk, and drawn from the breasts of this present world.

5. Lastly, The Lord doth it to beat down our pride, and keep us humble; we
should

and Pray. 107

should else be too much lifted up through our continued spiritual prosperity; and thus it was with *Paul*, 2 *Cor.* 10.7,8.

This Doctrine may afford us this useful Application,

By way of
{
1. Information.
2. Reprehension.
3. Examination.
4. Consolation.
5. Exhortation.
}

First, Information.

It may inform us, (1.) Of the Devils enmity, who is so much the Saints foe, as that he will not let them be quiet: This old Serpent, at first, deceived *Adam*, and deprived him of Paradise; yea, and ever since he hath been, and still is very busie to dispossess the Saints, if possible, of their spiritual Paradise.

2. We may learn hence the remaining seeds of corruptions that are in the best of Saints; without which (as I noted before) the Devil would always tempt in vain. 3. We

3. We may perceive what is the Saints state here below: it hath indeed many fair, pleasant prospects to the Christian eye, (I mean the eye of Faith) but the way is a tempted, troublesome, dangerous way, *Acts* 14, 22.

4. It may teach us the wisdom of God, and his great care of the Saints, who makes use of Satans enmity, and our corruptions, to do us good withall.

Secondly, Reprehension.

And thus it reproves those who think it an easie matter, a thing of nothing, to be a Christian.

2. It reproves such who censure poor tempted, afflicted ones,

1. Under their temptations, though not overcome.

2. When fallen; and oh how rash, uncharitable, and unchristian-like are they!

3. It is an occasion of rebuke to those who think it strange, that either themselves or others should be tempted.

Thirdly,

Thirdly, Examination.

This in these particulars:
1. To examine who is the Tempter, according to page 2,3,4,5,6,7.
2. To examine the temptation. See pag. 8,9,10,11.
3. To examine the frame of our hearts under, whether we carry it lightly, and indifferently, or are grieved and troubled for them.

Fourthly, Consolation.

From these Arguments:
Arg. 1. A tempted condition is frequent among the Saints; yea, and so usual, that I may confidently question, whether ever he were truly a Saint that is not tempted; and for this assertion there's a cloud of Witnesses in Scripture; one in 1 *Cor.* 10. 13.
Arg. 2. God hath promised assistance to tempted ones, 2 *Cor.* 12. 9. *My Grace is sufficient for thee*, &c. God is as able

to help, as thou canst be weak when thou art tempted.

Arg. 3. Christ was tempted, that he might know how to succour those that are tempted, *Heb.* 2. 17, 18. Read from verse 9.

Arg. 4. It is a blessing, or a blessed thing to endure temptation, *Jam.* 1. 12. and 5. 11.

Arg. 5. The Saints temptations are needful for them, 1 *Pet.* 1. 6. Thou canst not be without them.

Arg. 6. They are but for the trial of faith, 1 *Pet.* 1. 7. *James* 1. 3, 4. And should we be grieved that our faith is proved? The Goldsmith rather useth, then avoideth the fire, for the trying his Gold, Neither is the Gold diminished, but rather its worth more fully known, when the dross is gone. This is the tryal that doth try all the faith of every Child of God.

Arg.

Arg. 7. God hath promised, The burden shall not be too great for us to bear, 1 *Cor.* 10.13. this is ground of comfort, to know we shall not be over-matched by the temptation.   But

Arg. 8. A great comfort it is, that God thinks upon us at such a time; we are sure of this, both because of the temptations, and also the support we have under them.

Arg. 9. It is a great sign of Gods love, else he would never take care to try and purge us.

Arg. 10. Many times it goes before some signal Providence. And we may take it as a great sign, that God is about to do some great thing for us, or we must be employed in some great work for him: Thus he did with *Israel*, proved them forty years, before he gave them to possess the Land.

Arg. 11. Be not disconsolate; strong and

and long enduring temptations, when meeting with resistance, are a strong Argument of a strong Faith, and especially of the growth and encrease of faith. But (to be brief)

Arg. 12. Consider, the Saints condition here, is not their best state. There's Heaven to come yet, where there's no Tempter.

Arg. 13. We have not been so much, nor so often tempted, as we our selves have tempted God.

Arg. 14. The Devils temptations, though they be evils, yet are not the Saints evils, unless they be overcome by them.

Arg. 15. It is a great sign, as of Gods love, so of Satans hatred, and so consequently a token that thou art none of his, but Gods; else he would never rage thus. The Devil makes no such do with wicked ones.

Arg.

Arg. 16. As our temptations now abound, so shall our joy (in time) much more abound.

Many Arguments for Consolation I might make use of, and much more enlargement upon these, all which (for brevity sake) I here omit.

Fifthly, Exhortation.

1. Beware how you tempt the Devil, to tempt you; how you give an occasion by indulging any sin or lust.
2. When you are tempted, be not cowardly, but couragious; do not flye, but resist, *James* 4. 7.
3. Beware of pride, when delivered out of temptation; this may make us fall into a dangerous relapse.

Having finished this point, I proceed to shew in the next Observation, How we may avoid the evil of Temptation.

Doct. 2. *The only way to avoid the evil of Temptation, is to watch and pray*

In the handling of this Doctrine, we may consider these four things:
1. What it is to *Watch*.
2. What it is to *Pray*.
3. The proof of the point.
4. How *watching* and *praying* may conduce to our escape from the evil of *Temptation*.

Concerning the duty of *Watching* observe,

 First, What *Watching* implies
 Secondly, How we may do to Watch.

First, *Watching* implies,
1. A continual waking, like the Spouse, *Cant.* 5.2.
2. A diligent hearkening. Thus the Watch-man, *Isa.* 21.7.
3. A constant readiness; so *Peter* exhorts under a Metaphorical expression 1 *Pet.*1.13. *Gird up your loins*, i. e. Be

ready; it is taken from the *Jews* long garments, which they used to gird up about them, that they might run with less interruption.

Secondly, How we may do to watch; I shall but name the particulars.

1. Let the heart be continually fixed upon God: Oh! how will this cool our affections to the world, and kindle the fire of love to God!

2. Let the eye be much upon self: This will keep us low in spirit; *And blessed are the poor in spirit, for theirs is the Kingdom of Heaven,* Matt. 3.

3. Beware of drowsiness; we should shake it off by prayer.

4. Be well resolved in spirit; mind that of the Prophet, *King.* 18.21.

5. Be sure all be well within; be sure thy foundation be Christ; let there be no sin unrepented of, that will breed sorrow; Harbour no Enemy, no lust in the soul, *Prov.* 20.9.

6. Trust not thine (no, no not thine own) heart, but regulate it by the word of God; for the heart is deceitful, *Jer.* 17.9.

17. 9. And he is a fool that trusts his heart, *Prov.* 28. 26.

7. Keep therefore a narrow eye to the heart, *Prov.* 4. 23.

8. Call thy heart often to a strict account, *Psal.* 4. 4. Examine diligently, What have I done? What do I now? What am I about to do?

9. And if there be any thing out of order, tarry not, but repair it suddenly, Lay sin upon Christ, and then mourn over it.

10. Let nothing be suggested, and presently entertained, but first brought to tryal: See if it be the will of God, if it be for his glory; if it be not for his glory, it is not his will, &c.

11. Be sure to keep Conscience clear; a little filth (here) stops all the Channel, It is dangerous to know of (but one sin, and not confess it; much more dangerous to know thy sin, and wink at it.

12. For this end, keep an open ear to Conscience, let it speak.

13. Let the mouth be stopped to sin, and the hands tyed from wickedness

David

David prays that a watch may be set to the door of his lips; and certainly it is very needful.

14. Let the whole Armour of God be on, *Eph.* 6. 10, to 18.

Thus much concerning *Watching*, now concerning *Prayer*.

Consider,
First, What Prayer is.
Secondly, The several kinds of Prayer.
Thirdly, The manner how we are to Pray.

1. Prayer is the outward enlargement of the souls inward breathings; it is a work of Gods Spirit, and so flows out of the spirit and heart of man, *Zech.* 12. 10. *Rom.* 8. 26, 27. *Jude* 20. 1 *Cor.* 14. 15. *Psal.* 62. 8. and 42. 4. Prayer is a talking of the heart and soul with God, and of such a heart as is prepared by God, *Jer.* 29. 13. *Psal.* 27. 8. *Psal.* 10. 17.

2. And thus it is either mental, in the

heart,

heart only, *Exod.* 14. 15. 1 *Sam.* 1. 13. or else vocal, uttered by the voice, *Psal.* 77. 1. Again, this is secret prayer, when we pray alone; Thus *Daniel* did, when he set open his Windows, *Dan.* 6. 10, 11 Or more publike, when we pray with others in the Family, Congregation, &c. And here let some preparatives to prayer be added.

First, Pray, that you may pray; lift up your eye and your heart to God, when about to pray; thus did *David*, *Psal.* 141. 1, 2.

Secondly, Meditate,

1. On Gods Sufficiency, and especially his Promises, *Psal.* 50. 15. *Matth.* 7. 7. this will make confident in prayer.

2. On thine own wants and vileness, that thou mayest be fervent: So did *Ezra* 9. 6, 7.

3. On the great Majesty of God, to beget humility and lowliness of Spirit, *Eccles.* 5. 2. *Gen.* 32. 9, 10.

4. On the relation thou standest in to God, by Christ, as thy Father.

Thirdly,

Thirdly, Now how we are to pray.

1. We must pray what we understand, and understand what we pray, 1 Cor. 14. 15.

2. We must pray in the holy Spirit, be directed by it, *Jude* 20. *Rom.* 8. 26.

3. In the Name and Mediation of Christ, *i. e.* Relying upon the Merits of his, not our own righteousness. *John* 14. 13, 14. *John* 16. 23.

4. With Faith, believingly, that God will give us what is good for us. *Jam.* 1. 6, 7.

5. With Humility, and acknowledgment of our own unworthiness, *Psa.* 10. 17.

6. With an heart willing to be cleansed by the blood of Christ, *Jam.* 4. 6. From every polution, *Heb.* 10. 12. *Ps.* 66. 18.

7. With love to the Saints. *Mat.* 6. 14. 15.

8. With Zeal and Fervency, *James* 5. 16.

9. Do

9. Do not give off, but wrestle with God for a blessing with unwearied constancy, *Luke* 18. 1, to 9. *Mat.* 15.

10. Pray for heavenly things, first, and most: seek earthly things in the second place; the one absolutely, the other conditionally, *Mat.* 6. 33.

11. Pray for things agreeable to God, 1 *John* 5. 14. *Mat.* 20. 21, 22.

12. Take heed you love not long prayers, and think to be heard because they are long, *Mat.* 6. 7.

Now I come to the proof of this point; that the onely way to avoid the evil of temptation, is to watch and pray. This is clearly stated in the Text; so that it scarce needs more confirmation; onely take that of *Paul*, when buffeted by temptation, *for this*, saith he, *I besought the Lord thrice*, 2 *Cor.* 12. 8. Theres great need of watching and prayer.

1. Before we fall into temptation.

2. When we are under temptation. How watching and prayer conduceth

duceth to the anticipating the assaults of Satan, frustrating temptation.

First of all, for Watching.

1. It sets us in a readiness for an assault. When we are expecting, we shall not be taken unprovided.
2. It adds resolution, to stand it out against Satan. We know suddenness strikes us into a fear; when expectation, and deliberatiton, increaseth courage.
3. It is a Countermine to all Satans stratagems. It will deceive the Deceiver, to find us watching with spiritual diligence, when he would have us sleeping in carnal security.
4. Watching secures us from much evil that might be added, in case we were drawn, to the temptation. For security is no better then a temptation, especially at such a time.

Secondly, for prayer; This conduceth, to avoid the evil of temptation; because it fetcheth help from God, in whom is
all

all our strength: for it is Gods promise, *Call upon me in the day of trouble: I will deliver thee, and thou shalt glorifie me, Psal. 50. 15.* It is a great comfort, under temptation, to have a God to go to; especially, one that is able, and willing to help.

This may instruct us.

1. Then there is great need of watching. It is certainly an universal, necessary duty for all Saints, at whatever time, to watch. So saith Christ our Saviour, *What I say unto you, I say unto all, Watch, Mark 13. 37.* The great end of this duty, is the coming of the Lord Jesus. *Watch,* saith Christ, *for ye know not what hour your Lord doth come, Mat. 24, 42, 44.* there are three considerations may move us to watch.

1. Let us consider whom we offend and dishonour by our neglect in watching: No less then God. And would we, rather then want a nap of security, displease our God? Is God no more worth

worth to us, then so? Let us seriously weigh, how great an offence, how great a dishonour to God, our unwatchfulness is; and this will engage us to watch.

2. Let us consider whom we gratifie and advantage by our neglect; no less an enemy than Satan, the enemy of our souls. And shall we pleasure our grand Adversary? Oh no! then let us watch.

3. Whom we displeasure: it is our selves. And will we, that our souls should be losers? If not; let us be much, yea, always upon our watch.

But Secondly, It may inform us of the necessity of praying at all times. *Pray without ceasing.* 1 *Thes.* 5. 17. So *David* would pray and cry aloud, *at evening, at morning, and at noon. Psal.* 55. 17. And *Daniel prayed thrice a day, Dan.* 6. 16. It is the duty of all, and every Saint, in all conditions: In spiritual things;

1. Pray for grace, that God would give and encrease it, either in thy self, or others.

2. Pray

2. Pray against sin: against the guilt of sin, against the power of sin.

3. Pray against Satans Temptations.

1. Against the occasion of Temptation. That, if it be possible, thou mayest shun and escape the very appearance of it.

2. That the strength of corruption within, and the power of temptation without, may not be so prevalent as to lead thee captive to evil.

3. Pray, that the entrance into temptation, may be no disadvantage to thy grace; and that the escape out, may be no impeachment to, but rather for the advancement of Gods glory.

1. Pray for nothing, but what thou standest in need of. Unnecessary things are not to be the subject of our petitions. And therefore our Saviour bids us pray for our daily bread. And so that good man *Agur*, *Give me neither poverty nor riches*, *Proverbs* 30. 7, 8. 9.

2. Even in these things, pray with submissi-

submission to the will of God.

3. If watching and prayer be the means to escape the evil of temptation; then the strength of a Saint is not sufficient. No, we must go to God for deliverance.

4. If we do not watch and pray, all other ways and means are irregular at least, if not sin.

Thus much for Information, Now for Exhortation.

1. Watch and Pray continually; but especially at a time of temptation.

2. Be serious in watching and prayer; some do it between hot and cold, or by fits, or with much lightness of spirit. But saith the Apostle, *Be sober, and Watch unto Prayer.* Sobriety, Seriousness becomes those that call upon God.

The End of the Third Sermon.

CONSIDERATIONS OF Death:

Containing some few Reasons why men fear it; and opposite Reasons by way of Answer, why they should not fear it.

Obj. 1. First, Because thereby we are deprived of the exercise of all our sences; so that whatever Delight either our Tast, Smell, Hearing, Sight, or Feeling hath afforded us, we shall enjoy the same no more; whilest (perhaps) many Generations after us shall

shall have the fruition thereof.

Anf. First, As the exercise of our Sences afford opportunity of Delight, so are they thereby capable of annoying and grieving us; as, the Taft, by bitterness and sharpness, &c. the Smell, by noisom polution, corruption, &c. The Hearing, by terrible and hideous noise, and evil tidings. The Sight, By loathsome affrighting, and miserable appearances. The Feeling, by tedious pains, &c.

Again, We have had the benefit of surviving former Generations, who were lyable to what we are; and so shall be those who shall succed us.

Obj. 2. But that which aggravates the evil hereof, is, a mans being cut off in the flower or strength of his Age; whereas if he live the common Age of man, he should the more contentedly leave this life.

Anf.

Answ. VVhy, What is man? Is he not a flower, and as grafs, and the like? and are they not cut off in their beft eftate? and may not God when he walketh in, or vieweth his Garden of humane flowers, have as much liberty to cropp them, as men have of theirs? furely yea: for all are his.

Secondly, And though God permit fome men to live as long as an ordinary courfe of nature, oft be it, feventy years, (which is judged the moft common) or more; yet he hath not promifed them fo long life.

Thirdly, And though fome live fo long, yet confidering the VVarres, and Plauges, and other difeafes among men, it is not without reafon thought there are many more dye, who have not lived according to the courfe of nature

Fourthly, As we conclude that no perfon better, or fo well as the Gardener, or fuch as fowed, planted, dressed, and frequently practiseth about the flowers and plants, knows when and for what reason to gather and pluck up; so no person knows better nor so well as God knows, when to cut or pluck up what he hath planted in the world, who doth all his actions upon good and weighty reasons, even greater and better than any Gardener or other person hath for what he doth in his concernment.

Object. 3. In death a man becomes a lothsome spectacle to all beholders, insomuch that the sight and smell of the survivers find not more noysome offence from, and account not more vilely of the most lothsome creatures in the world, then of a dead and rotten Corps of Mankind; and is not that very grievous, to become from a delightfull Companion an abhorrence of all people?

Answ. 1. True, Being dead a man

man becomes a lothsome spectacle to all beholders. And do not many diseases to which a man is incident in his life, effect the same in beholders?

2. Though man do become by death, what is suggested; yet hath he then no sence thereof; and in that is the Proverb verified, (*What the Eye sees not, the Heart rues not*;) for look on man in that case (as we may) as a dead lump of Corruption, and what of misery can we apply thereto? who looks on a Dunghil, or a Jakes, and saith, Alas, for its misery? the same feels not, and knows not any: So that although the thoughts of such a condition by Death, grieves us whilst living, yet in that condition it self, we shall be free from such grief.

3. Again, Consider that we were but earth before we had life; and being dead, we return to our first estate, and though withall, we become for a season more impure and cor-

rupt then barely earth, yet in time we shall become very dust, when the putrefaction is consumed; and in that sence (but especially in a more excellent) will that saying be fulfilled, *viz.* Corruption shall put on Incorruption.

Object. 4. Death deprives man of his society, with whom he hath had sweet converse.

Answ. 1. True, but it is in order (if he dye in Gods favour) to enjoy in due season, better society then men on earth have.

2. Besides, as thou loosest thy friends on earth, so thou art rid of thy enemies there too.

Object. 5. Though death may make way for better society then we have been used to here, yet who knows when it shall be, the Body not being to receive new life, till the General

ral Resurrection, which may be very long first?

Answ. Suppose it be so (as the most Christians believe) that the best part of man receives glory and happiness immediately after death; yet from the time of Death, to the general resurrection (at which time all knowing Christians believe the reward of the Righteous will not fail) the space betwixt Death and it, is but as one day; as he who by means of Apoplexy or like occasion, sleeps many days and nights without wakeing, cannot esteem of the time; he has slept answerable to the measure thereof: But it may be to him as one day or one night, and in this sence may Death be reckoned (as usually in the holy Scripture it is) a sleep.

object. 6. Suppose a man should dye by the hand of a cruel Man-slayer, who delights in torturing and destroying the body of man, as hath been seen; would not the conceit of one so cruel, coming to act his mind upon a person, make the thoughts of such a death very terrible, when therein a man is no more regarded then a dog, or the vilest creature?

Ans. 1. Yea: But do not many by reason of wounds and Gangreen'd Members in their life, for preserving the body, Limb or Member, endure as great pain, and tremble as much at the sight of the Chyrurgion, when he comes to do his office on them, as a man doth at the sight of the Executioner to do his? And consider, that all that is commonly done at such death, causeth less pain to the party, then what some do suffer by the cutting off one limb, or curing some one wound or disease.

2. Again, Consider, That the more of torment a man endures in this life, whether at death, or otherwise, the less he is like to suffer after this life,

life, and the more bleſſing he is likely then to enjoy, if he be a good, or worthy man, ſuffering here as a child of God, and not a Reprobate. *Revel.* 18. Verſe 7. Chapter 20. Verſe 4, 5, 6.

Object. 7. But in our preſent Eſtate, we have Being, Life, Senſe and Reaſon; and in Death, we ſhall have (at the moſt) onely Being, and is not that very grievous to conſider, that we ſhall be reduced to no better a condition than a piece of earth or a ſtone?

Anſw. It is true, that the conſideration thereof is very grievous in it ſelf; but yet whilſt man hath Reaſon, as well as Being, Life, and Sence; Let him uſe it to conſider alſo, that he hath no more cauſe to complain, then for a piece of the earth he now treads on, if it ſhould pleaſe God (as at the firſt) to create thereof a man like himſelf, and ſhortly reduce

duce it to its former state; for thus it is now with mankind in general.

Object. 8. It's confest, that there is a Proverb, [For one Pleasure, a thousand Dollers] but it seems to be no better then a flourish of learned men, to colour over a bad matter: For although the miseries of man in this life are many; yet if the benefits therein did not surmount those miseries, it is likely that men would not so much desire to continue therein, as now they do; and therefore who would not fear Death?

Answ. 1. Suppose it be granted, that the Proverb is but a flourish, and that the benefits of this Life do surmount the miseries thereof; yet no man is able to say how long a person in order to be happy, should live here to enjoy those benefits; But God he knows, and he hath appointed for men once to dye, there-

therefore rest satisfied in his wisdom for disposing of thy time for Death, concluding, that the same shall be in its due season.

2. Again Consider, that it is Gods Prerogative over all his creatures, to dispose of them how, and when he will.

3. Moreover God hath already set the bounds of thy life, beyond which thou canst not pass; wherefore patiently commit thy self to him in well-doing, and quietly satisfie thy self with his pleasure, making of necessity a vertue; for it is in vain for a man to strive against the stream, by tormenting himself with that which he cannot avoid; yet this doth not hinder that all men may (yea ought to) use what lawfull means God gives them opportunity of; for saving their lives.

Object. 2.

Object. 9. Well, though it be granted that these answers which have been urged, have (most, if not all of them) common reason, and experience on their side: yet there remains further ground to fear death, as well from what the holy Scripture, as Nature or Custome doth evidence, and that in part is this. *Viz.* Death is reckoned the King of Terrors, as in *Job* 18. 14. compared with *Heb.* 2. 15.

Answ. Death is indeed granted to be the King of Terrors, but that is in regard of a certain Sting that is in it; if that Sting be taken away, Death will not be so terrible as before, yea it will be rather gain then loss to dye, if that sting reach not the party dying.

Object. 10. I confess, there may seem to be some comfort in that answer, if one knew how to escape that Sting; But that is a thing so diffi-

DEATH. 139

difficult, that I greatly fear Death; If I were sufficiently provided in that case, I should have comfort.

Answ. It's true, that the difficulty lyes even there, where it is exprest; but though it be so difficult, yea, impossible with man, yet it is not so difficult with God, he hath sufficiently provided for man in that case; for he that is King of Kings, hath subdued that King of Terrors, and done what is needfull for man concerning the same; for which purpose see these Scriptures, *viz.* 1 *Cor.* 15. 55, 56. 57. *John* 3. 14, 15, 16, 17, and part of the 18. *Rom.* 5. to 12. and forward to the end of the Chapter.

Object. 11. I grant, it appears plain enough, that there is through Jesus Christ victory wrought over that enemy mentioned, and answerably the Sting is taken away that I feared; I say, taken away for some, but it seems not for all, because it is said, *The Sting*

Sting of Death is Sin, so that where sin is, there the Sting is also, and I know my self a Sinner, therefore in danger of that Sting.

Answ. Indeed if thou knowest thy self a sinner, and grievest not for it, but art therewith content, neither repenting of, nor reforming from it; I cannot say the Sting of Death is taken away for thee; but if thou dost truly repent of thy sin, and indeavour with thy heart to forsake sin, the Sting of Death is taken away for thee; for the Scripture tells us Christ dyed for sinners, that is to say, for humble penitent sinners, not for obstinate ones: A notable example whereof was manifested when the Saviour of the world himself was held up, *Viz.* In that of the two Theives, the one rayled on Christ, and was reproved; the other humbled himself, he also prayed, and received the answer of Salvation.

Object. 12.

Object. 12. Indeed that Example (methinks) doth tend to prove what you say; but in so considerable a case as this, a man would desire more than one Witness.

Answ. Therefore take more, *Viz.* Proverbs 8. 13. *Isaiah* 1. from verse 16 to verse 19. *Matthew* 9, verse 12, 13. *Romans* 5. verse 8. 1 *Tim.* 1. 15, 16.

Some further GROUNDS, whereon a poor Sinner may expect Mercy, through the Merits of Jesus Christ.

1. Through a sense of sin, so to look on the Lord Christ, as those who were stung with Scorpions in the Wilderness, did on the brazen Serpent.

2. Next followeth humbling of the soul, the effect of which is to be seen in these Scriptures, *viz. Job* 22. ver. 29. *Psal.* 10. ver. 17. *Isa.* 55. ver. 15. *Jam.* 4. 6.

Which Humiliation begets a self-Examination, by which knowing the Holy Rule of Life, and comparing a mans life to that Rule, trying how his

his case is, he is thereby ready to say (in respect to his misery) as the Apostle doth, *Rom.* 7. verse 9, 10, 11. sees himself a dead man in the sense of the Law.

Then that works in him, a Holy sorrow, and that a repentance not to be repented of; *Viz.* Repentance to Salvation, 2 *Cor.* 7. 10, 11.

It brings him to see, not only that he is a condemned or guilty person, but that he is irrecoverably lost, must needs perish, without some Person as Mediator or Redeemer, do undertake for his Ransom, or hath undertaken it; for that God is infinitely just, and he must have his Justice satisfied; and all that the poor soul can do, is but to amend his life for the future, walking more conformable to the Righteous law of God, then heretofore. But alas! That is no more then what ought to be, for the time to come it will not satisfie Divine Justice
for

for the Transgressions already done against the Law of God, any more then a mans paying another an ensuing Week, Month or Year, for all he is engaged for within that space of time, doth satisfie or clear the Debt which became due in time before that week: neither (indeed) can a man, of himself, satisfie for what he shall owe to it, in the remaining part of his life. Now this consideration works the soul into a melting frame, brings him on his knees, to say, as the poor Publican, Lord, have mercy on me a sinner: And, as the prodigal humbled, and sees all his rambling shifts in vain, for yielding him that solid comfort, his soul thirsteth after, therefore resolves to go home to his Father, and although he may look upon him as enraged against him (for which his soul knew there was just cause) yet he goes humbling himself to his father, saying, *Father I have sinned, &c. and am no more worthy to be called thy Son.* Now observe

serve the succeſs; *When he was yet a great way off, his father saw him, and had compaſſion, and fell on his neck and kiſſed him;* And farther, entertained him, not as a ſervant as he humbly beſought (*for the humble ſhall be exalted*) but as a Son, and rejoiced in him. *Luke* 15.

The *Aſſyrians* alſo well knew what good this humble Application vvas likely to effect in an *Iſraelitiſh* King; (1 *Kings* Chap. 20. verſe 31, 32.) and, if mercy may be expected from one of thoſe Kings, then much more may it be from the Supreim, the King of thoſe Kings, the Almighty, who hath promiſed large grace to humble ſouls.

So *Heſter* (at the advice of *Mordecai* Chap. 4. 5. made good proof of this humble way of addreſſing for Mercy, in a caſe otherwiſe deſperate, the ſucceſs whereof was that Royal Scepter held forth, with Grace,

L to

to grant even beyond the Petition, though she knew not when she went about it, but that she should perish, yet wisely perceiving that she must perish, if she had not so applyed, she proceeded.

Thus was it with the Lepers, 2 *Kings* 7. 4. If they went into the City, they should suffer Famine; if they staid where they were, they must die; they therefore would venture for releif amongst their enemies, being sure they could not be worse then they were: They could but die one way or another. So, when the Soul is thus brought to see its misery, and humbles it self thoroughly, withall is willing to embrace what means soever represents so much as a possibility of saving it; then God shews his mercy to refresh it, according to that 57 Chap. of *Isa.* verse 15, 16. &c. to revive the spirit of the humble, and to revive the heart of the contrite ones: So *Psalm* 51. 15.

15. *Ezekiel* 33. 11. and forward. And Christ comfortably invites such a poor sinner that is weary and heavy laden with the sense of his sin, he invites him to come and receive rest; and thus the Gospel doth in general, give encouragement to humble, penitent sinners to expect Salvation from the eternal God; the sting before spoken of being taken away.

Then being truly humbled under the sense of that miserable condition which sin hath made a man liable to, and being rightly desirous of Salvation; that which is required of him, is, only to believe that the Righteous God, who might have made him eternally miserable; hath, notwithstanding through his tender compassion (his Mercy being above all his works) resolved on a way to satisfie his Justice, by acquitting the Guilty, who was no way able to pay a sufficient ransom for his own Redemption, therefore provided a price

price satisfactory, to redeem poor fallen man from the curse; concerning which, both the Prophets and Apostles have witnessed, as in *Isaiah* 53. and 55. Chapters. *Micah*, Chap. 5. verse 2. *Hosea*, Chap. 11. verse 1. *Psalm* 22. *Acts*, Chap. 1. verse 8. Chap. 10. verse 41. And more Scriptures; that price of Salvation, being Jesus Christ, of whom the Angels proclaime, about the time of his entrance into the VVorld; *Glory be to God in the Highest; on Earth, Peace, Good-will towards men,* Luke, Chapter 2, and the 14 verse, And the Evangelist, *John*, Chapter 3. and the 16 verse, declares positively, That *God so loved the VVorld, that he gave his onely begotten Son, That whosoever believeth in him, should not perish, but have eternal life.*

There is the term of Salvation, *viz.* Believing in his Son, to be that Gift and Ransome, which the

the Gospel generally holds forth to those vvho vvould knovv vvhat they should do to be saved. Withall, there must be an obedient Conversation, and that universally, to all Gods Commandments, answerable to a poor souls ability, so long as life may last.

FINIS.

www.ingramcontent.com/pod-product-compliance
Lightning Source LLC
LaVergne TN
LVHW061215060426
835507LV00016B/1946